The Path

THE
PATH
A GUIDE TO
HAPPINESS

Khenpo Sherab Zangpo

WISDOM PUBLICATIONS
199 Elm Street
Somerville, MA 02144 USA
wisdompubs.org

© 2017 Khenpo Sherab Zangpo
All rights reserved.

No part of this book may be reproduced in any form or by any means,
electronic or mechanical, including photography, recording, or by any
information storage and retrieval system or technologies now known or
later developed, without permission in writing from the publisher.

Library of Congress Cataloging-in-Publication Data is available.

LCCN 2017018044

ISBN 978-1-61429-415-3   ebook ISBN 978-1-61429-423-8

21 20 19 18 17
5 4 3 2 1

Cover design by Jim Zaccaria.
Set in Baskerville 9.5/ 15.

Wisdom Publications' books are printed on acid-free paper and meet the
guidelines for permanence and durability of the Production Guidelines
for Book Longevity of the Council on Library Resources.

♻ This book was produced with environmental mindfulness.
For more information, please visit wisdompubs.org/wisdom-environment.

Printed in the United States of America.

Please visit fscus.org.

Contents

Editor's Preface

At some point of our life, we have all asked ourselves what it takes to be happy—and many of us spend so much time investigating this question. In this book, Khenpo Sherab Zangpo offers us valuable assistance.

Khenpo Sherab Zangpo is a lineage-holder in the Tibetan Buddhist tradition of the Great Perfection and a heart-son of His Holiness Jigme Phunstok Rinpoche, one of the most influential Buddhist leaders of our time and one who ushered in a renaissance of Tibetan Buddhism in Tibet in the 1980s. Khenpo, a tireless teacher and writer, is the author of several highly acclaimed books in Chinese, but *The Path: A Guide to Happiness* is his first book published in English. In it he offers theory and practical advice, showing readers how the teachings of the Buddha lead to lasting happiness through training and transforming our minds.

What makes the book especially compelling is the way Khenpo blends together the timeless wisdom of Buddhism with his own compassionate appreciation of today's life, making the teachings both close to our life and practical to our daily problems and mental perplexity. The book is fascinating to read, in part because of the way Khenpo illustrates the teachings with experiences from his own life and with endearing stories about the remarkable teachers he has met, including His Holiness Jigme Phuntsok Rinpoche.

It is our hope that this warm and beautifully written book may help readers achieve not only long-sought happiness but also lasting happiness as well.

We would like to dedicate to Khenpo the following verse from

The Path

"The Long-Life Prayer for Khenpo Sherab Zangpo" written by His
Holiness Kyabgon Gongma Trichen Rinpoche:

> To Amitayus of the Buddha of Immeasurable Life, master
>   of the ten powers,
> To Padmasambhava of Guru Oddiyana Vajradhara, realizer
>   of the five wisdoms,
> We pray for the blessing nectar rain of fortune, longevity
>   and wisdom,
> Always bestowed by you and falling swiftly like water
>   running off a deep cliff.
> Sherab Zangpo, the holder of the Tripitaka, the very
>   essence of Buddha's words,
> Help beings dispel their darkness of ignorance and
>   delusion.
> He is the source of all virtues and good qualities, and shines
>   like a hundred thousand suns together.
> May this sun-like teacher, who is wise, disciplined and kind,
>   long remain.
> He the noble one is like the eye of the world, possessing
>   transcendental wisdom and connecting people in all
>   directions,
> To enlighten them and lead them to liberation just like the
>   sun making a hundred petals of a lotus open.
> May obstacles impeding the longevity of this great teacher
>   be removed speedily,
> And his kind deeds and merits continue shining in every
>   corner of the four continents.

PART 1

Life in the Eyes of a Buddhist

Happiness

One of my students once asked me how to be happy, and I thought the question was easy to answer: by letting go of attachment one achieves happiness. But over time I found that such a straightforward answer does not work for everyone. What exactly is attachment? How do we let go of it? These are issues worthy of further examination. So when I face the same question nowadays, I reply by asking, "How are you feeling right now?" Happiness, after all, is one's state of mind.

Sometimes people are not unhappy, but they perceive themselves as being that way. If you observe how your mood changes over time, you will find that emotions affecting your mood are like clouds—changeable and easy to disperse. From afar, clouds can appear solid as if you could walk on them. But if you reached them, of course you could not. Even so, clouds often build up in the sky. Likewise, emotional clouds too often gather in us to shape our state of mind. If our emotions are dominated by positive ones like joy and contentment, we feel happy.

What brings happiness? The relief of pain and suffering makes us happy. Do not regard happiness as something that can only be achieved through daunting effort. Happiness is discoverable anywhere, even in the life of an ordinary person. A drink makes you happy when you are thirsty. A hearty meal makes you happy when you are hungry. A seat to sit on while riding the subway makes you happy after a long, exhausting day. And the extraction of a decaying tooth makes you happy if you have been suffering from a toothache for days.

3

Happiness can also be a cool breeze on a summer night, or the shade of a tree that shelters you from the scorching sun. Happiness can even be found in the simplicity of a single breath. Meditating on one's own breath is a common technique taught to beginners. By mentally following each round of inhalation and exhalation in quiet awareness, we try to bring our mind to a neutral and tranquil state, which allows us to experience inner bliss. Sometimes, happiness is delivered by the most modest changes in our lives. The respiratory symptoms associated with the common cold such as nasal congestion or a runny nose can be maddening—after experiencing them, just being able to breathe normally can generate a sense of relief so powerful it borders on joy.

Happiness is always close at hand, but we are either too restless to be aware of it, or it is too fleeting to be relished to the fullest. If we can look inward and observe our emotions and thoughts as much as we examine the blemishes on our faces, it will not be difficult to sense the happiness present in every moment. If we do not entrust happiness solely to the ephemeral pleasures and thrills that the material world brings, our sense of happiness can be both extended and expanded.

The root of our unhappiness, as the Buddha says, comes from attachment—attachment to a self and attachment to things around us. We believe in an inherently existent self—this is my physical body, my idea, my house, my friend, and so on—but that belief is a miscomprehension of our true nature. The second-century Indian Buddhist master Nagarjuna's *Fundamental Verses of the Middle Way* and the eighth-century Indian Buddhist master Shantideva's *The Way of the Bodhisattva* provide detailed instructions on how to eliminate the attachment to a self. In short, there is no such self that exists intrinsically from the Buddhist point of view.

Is the person you see in the mirror every morning really you? A biology teacher will tell you that our bodies undergo constant metabolism, which leads to the continuous death and renewal of many of our cells Moreover, your image in the mirror changes constantly. If friends who have not seen you for decades meet you again, they may hardly recognize you at first sight. The only reason that they can still identify you is that you do not exist in isolation and your associations with them and the world around you leave traces that connect your past with the present. After all, nobody in this world comes out of a void. Our relativity—our links with people and the environment—is what allows us to be identified and recognized. Once we see such relativity, we will start to understand the pointlessness of building a wall between the outer world and ourselves. The sense of frustration induced by the futility of doing so can only make us unhappy.

Not only do we misread the dynamics between the outer world and ourselves, but we also know little about our inner world. For many, the strangest person in the world is oneself, and we rarely make efforts to understand ourselves better: How do I feel right now? Am I full or hungry, cold or hot, tired or energetic, peaceful or restless? Interestingly, not everyone can answer these seemingly simple questions instantly due to our lack of mindfulness and awareness of our present state. It is ironic that, in an era of information, we may know a lot about the US presidential election but little about our own physical and emotional experiences and wants. Our minds are too scattered to take the opportunity to know ourselves better. To gain and maintain moment-to-moment mindfulness, the practice of the four foundations of mindfulness is taught in an early Buddhist scripture: mindfulness of the body, mindfulness of feelings or sensations, mindfulness of consciousness, and mindfulness of the things around us. Through these four kinds of mindfulness, many negative emotions can be relieved. Perhaps some of you have had this experience: As you feel a physical pain, you mentally focus on the pain and observe it—its location, its extent, its intensity, and so on. After a short while, you notice that the pain starts to ease. When you are troubled by negative emotions

5

like anger, jealousy, anxiety, or fear, try to watch them closely in a similar way.

Let us examine anger, which is the most harmful negative emotion. Before spiralling out of control, it has to go through a gradual process like a raging fire fanned by wind from tiny sparks. Many people will not notice the fire until it becomes uncontrollable. But if we pay closer attention, we can easily extinguish it at an early stage. Alternatively, we can also do nothing and simply watch how it develops. We might not know that we ourselves are often the ones that fuel the fire. Now that we are onlookers, the fire will eventually die down by itself.

Other kinds of emotions develop in a similar pattern. Rather than being pushed around by them, turn to face them and watch calmly from where they come and where they go. Nothing—including negative emotions—lasts forever. When you feel jealous, angry, worried, fearful, or wronged, just tell yourself it is no big deal. You cannot keep feeling angry or worried throughout your entire life, even if you want to.

We touched on the idea that there is no absolute boundary between oneself and the outer world. This connection gives us a chance to cultivate loving-kindness and compassion. We seek happiness and avoid pain. We like to be loved and cared for. If someone misunderstands us, we feel aggrieved. These are the sorts of desires and feelings shared by all sentient beings. On a busy street, we can meet different kinds of people who want happiness just as we do, although they might be clumsy in the way they seek it. Understanding this commonality helps us develop empathy and tolerance.

Being mindful of negative emotions rather than suppressing them can also help us develop compassion. When we are anxious, angry, jealous, or fearful, reflect on these emotions and think: there must be many other beings suffering just like me. For both them and myself, I must find a way to remove such suffering. Shantideva says that when we generate bodhichitta, the awakening mind, we are like an impoverished person who finds a gem in a garbage dump—it brings us endless joy and fulfills our wishes.

Another sign of not knowing ourselves is that we do not know how to treat ourselves fairly and live at peace with ourselves; we are instead self-indulging, self-demanding, or self-criticizing. We are always dissatisfied with what we have, such as our appearance, intelligence, social status, wealth, and living conditions. Consequently, we spend our whole lives attempting to make these things better. The Buddhist scriptures term the world in which we live *saha lokadhatu*— the world of endurance imperfect yet bearable. It is foolish and futile to look for perfection in this world. Yet so many people work hard just for material comfort and fortune at the expense of life's simple delights. And at the end of their days, happiness is still a distant dream.

A happy life must start with accepting imperfection: be content, appreciate an imperfect "I," and learn to say "I am happy with who I am and what I have." In this way, spiritual practice is not for us to acquire more skills or to become more attractive, more accomplished, more affluent, or more enviable. More often it is the other way around—a simple life with a contented mind is the goal. If we reflect deeply on our most basic attachments—even to people and things we generally consider vital to our happiness—we will see that none of them is indispensible to us. Looking outside of ourselves for happiness is like trying to quench one's thirst with salty water: the more we drink, the thirstier we get.

My late root teacher His Holiness Jigme Phuntsok Rinpoche once said, "Although not all of us can be like Jetsun Milarepa, who completely renounced mundane life, we can at least be less attached." Everything comes with a price, including wealth and status. The nineteenth-century master Patrul Rinpoche, even after becoming a prominent teacher, lived a simple life and traveled around unrecognized. One day on his daily round of alms giving, Rinpoche performed a transference ritual for someone who had recently passed away. When the auspicious signs of a favorable rebirth appeared after the ritual, the family of the deceased made an offering of three horses to Rinpoche as a token of gratitude. But Rinpoche, who looked rather shabby, refused, and said, "I do not want any offering. If you have three horses, you will have three horses' worth of trouble."

Some may say that Tibetans live a harsh life and that devotion to Buddhism fails to make their society more developed and their living more comfortable. We Tibetans, however, think differently. We define a developed society by its harmony and happiness, not by its material prosperity, for a rich life without joy is by no means a happy life. The Buddhist way of life is what allows us to achieve harmony and happiness.

It is said that Nagarjuna wished to be reborn to a middle-class family that was neither too poor nor too rich. He believed this would spare him from worrying about either the necessities of life or the temptations of material excess, creating an ideal circumstance for Buddhist practice. For the same reason, many Tibetans are happy for their entire lives despite having humble homes and modest resources. They understand that the inner joy nurtured by contentment surpasses even the pleasures enjoyed by Indra, the king of gods. Conventional thinking dictates that we must have many things to be happy. However, sudden tragedies like death, illness, or natural disasters remind us that we do not need much to be happy.

In addition, we often fail to recognize some of the basic and apparent features of the world, such as impermanence. Although all things in the universe change constantly, we instinctively seek security and become disillusioned as a result. Often such disillusionment and the frustration it brings are merely a reflection of our experience with impermanence. Once we understand and acknowledge impermanence as an inherent part of life, we will become less attached. Knowing that we are not the only ones who experience unfavourable situations and feel insecure, we will take things more lightheartedly. While still doing our best, we will realize that we cannot always get what we want and it is pointless to be anxious about failure. Doing so will by no means make us pessimistic, nor will it render our life meaningless. Sometimes we should even be thankful for impermanence, for it provides us a way out of suffering. We can always have a new beginning, a second chance, a wiser way to live happier, as we are doing now through Buddhism.

To help us subdue attachment further and attain happiness, we need to understand the other two important Buddhist concepts—causality and emptiness. I will elaborate on these two subjects in later chapters of this book.

Leaf Reading from the Jade Tree

Natural disasters can strike anywhere and anytime, and the damage and pain they inflict defies reason. It is for this reason that some of my students were puzzled when a magnitude-seven earthquake struck Yushu in 2010. Yushu—which means "jade tree" in Chinese—is a remote county in the ethnic Tibetan region of northwest China's Qinghai province, formerly known as the Kokonor region. My students not only wondered why natural disasters happen so often but also questioned why they occur even in places where the Buddhist faith and, supposedly, its blessings prevail. Unable to comprehend the fact that impermanence remains inexorable even through Buddhist practice, they hoped to find answers from me.

I felt the questions raised by my students largely reflected their lack of understanding of impermanence, a pervasive feature of all phenomena. To address these questions, it is necessary to start with impermanence—what it is and how we should understand it. Meanwhile, it would be helpful to look even deeper into the causes of natural disasters and determine how we can help when they happen, and, more importantly, what we should do in everyday life.

Impermanence

Disasters often strike suddenly, and we are usually caught off guard. Having heard about the teaching on impermanence, we know that everything is changing and both the gain and loss of life are unavoidable. But still we find it hard to accept the truth of impermanence when it is revealed in such a fierce way.

Impermanence often seems harsh because we only notice it when we suffer from severe pain, separation, or death. The Buddha taught that all things that arise dependently are impermanent. We can understand this truth intellectually, but when it comes to our daily experiences, we continue perceiving impermanence as unwanted or unexpected situations and events that cause frustration and agony.

After all, we are not humble enough, reluctant to drop our pride and prejudice and fully accept impermanence. If we regard some kinds of impermanence as advantageous, friendly, and acceptable while others not, we fail to grasp the meaning of the Buddha's teachings on impermanence. If we expect certain people, things, and phenomena to stay more constant, we also fail to understand the Buddha's teachings.

After the Yushu earthquake, some students asked me why the earthquake happened in an area where there are so many monasteries and almost everyone is Buddhist. Many of them thought, out of pure devotion, that all things related to Buddhism should be able to escape impermanence by some magic power. Apparently, people still prefer to believe in the existence of permanence. They expect that the people, things, and conditions they are fond of and familiar with will always remain satisfactory. Nonetheless, the Buddha wants us to understand that all things arising from causes and conditions are like a dream, a phantom, a dewdrop, a flash of lightning—none of them lasts. Even the Buddha himself became sick, grew old, and entered nirvana.

Ancient India's Nalanda Monastery was once a glorious center of Buddhist learning, attracting a large number of scholars in its heyday. Destroyed in the twelfth century, it is now a desolate place where only ruins remain. Likewise, the three-story main temple of Samye Monastery, the first Buddhist monastery built in Tibet and consecrated by the great Indian tantric Buddhist adept Padmasambhava, was destroyed overnight by a raging fire. Moreover, the splendid reliquaries built by King Ashoka in India more than two thousand years ago have now all disappeared without the faintest trace. Even the eighty-four thousand methods of Buddhadharma together with numerous scriptures will sink into oblivion one after another. The sublime teachings and their inconceivable blessings, which have benefited countless beings and guided them on the path to liberation, will be submerged in the flowing river of time.

Therefore, blessings from the Three Jewels—the Buddha, Dharma, and Sangha—are not meant to fortify our ego and reinforce our delusions about security. Nor do they serve as impenetrable armor to shield us from unwanted circumstances. If we think they do, we can only become more vulnerable in a world so fickle and unpredictable. The blessing power of the Three Jewels, in fact, concerns our mental transformation. Once we take refuge in the Three Jewels, their blessings are manifested in our increased kindness and wisdom, and in our further cultivation of bodhichitta and insight into emptiness. Nothing is more effective than bodhichitta and the view of emptiness to foster an open and resilient mind.

Some people observed that the Tibetans affected by the Yushu earthquake reacted in an unusual way. Ruins on the streets reminded people of the earthquake that had just happened, but an unusual sense of calmness permeated the town in the aftermath. People did not wail or shout. Instead, they worked hard to rescue and help each other. Young boys managed to get their grandmothers out of the debris by digging through the rubble with their bare hands. Men who just lost their families and houses walked a long way to help friends. Some would not talk about the loss of their relatives, but every night, before going to bed, they lay in their tents and silently recited scriptures. Each person grieved differently, and sorrow was quietly transformed by a pure wish to do what was possible to help the living and to benefit the rebirth of the dead. Most families lost their kin and belongings. Some even became penniless. Still they were sanguine about the future: "As long as others are getting better, we will, too."

Nurtured by Buddhism, many Tibetans on the plateau take impermanence as a fact of life. They do not expect that things should evolve as they wish. Those who are born will die; those who meet will part. Such is life. Whether they suffer from disasters or enjoy prosperity, behave with strength or weakness, refuse or accept the facts of human existence, life flows on inexorably.

The Buddha told a famous story about impermanence—the story of Kisa Gotami, a woman who was devastated after losing her only child. In her grief, she asked if anyone knew of a medicine that could bring her son back to life, but to no avail. Finally, she went to the Buddha for help. The Buddha said to her, "Yes, I can indeed help. But in order to prepare the medicine, you must first bring me some mustard seeds. These seeds have to be from a family that has not experienced a death within it."

With high hopes, Gotami went away. She went from house to house, but to her disappointment, she could not find a single house where no one had died. Eventually, the realization struck her that she was not the only one who suffered in this way. After she returned, the Buddha preached to her compassionately, "You thought you were the only one who suffered. The truth is that all things are impermanent."

There is not a single day when we do not live with impermanence and confront death and suffering, and I am not sure what sort of death and suffering can be called gentle. People often approach me for advice and consolation whenever their friends, relatives, or they themselves experience anguish in life. Almost every day I hear bad news of this sort. This allows me to gain insight into the suffering and impermanent nature of life. It also makes me realize the pressing need for spiritual practice.

At death, most people feel helpless and fearful regardless of how they are dying. Until then, their knowledge, skills, and intellectual capability are employed for mundane concerns, and they hardly ponder what death really means and how they should deal with it.

Even if one does not encounter any serious misfortunes, life is still fleeting, and the passage of decades is like the twinkling of an eye. When days sail too smoothly, it is easy for one to overlook aging and perhaps even death. Not only the young but also the old tend to have the false impression that life will go on indefinitely. I met Lama Regya of Tashi Monastery a few years ago. Although he was more than eighty years old, he still took his Dharma practice too causally. So I urged him to spend more time on practice because of the imminence of death. To my surprise, he died the same autumn. I trust that, given his lifelong Buddhist training, he could handle most circumstances in life calmly. But death is such a dramatic change that it induces strong fear and agony. I wondered how he faced it without sufficient preparation.

One particular issue of utmost importance for Tibetans is how to navigate the dying process peacefully without going astray in the intermediate state between death and rebirth. Only accomplished practitioners can face living and dying at ease and have control over their rebirth after death. Ordinary people tend to be engulfed by extreme agony at the moment of death, completely forgetting their usual practice. Unable to recognize various appearances in the intermediate state, they miss the precious chance for spiritual liberation. If, at this crucial moment, someone is at the side of a dying person—consoling and guiding him to overcome fear and to recognize the clear light of the mind or the pure realms of the buddhas—they will be liberated.

It is for this reason that all burial methods including sky burial and cremation come with special transference rituals and funeral arrangements in Tibet. Tibetans will have these transference rituals performed for their deceased relatives so that they can go through the critical intermediate states without obstacles. For Buddhists, to help their dear ones to gain liberation is the most meaningful thing they can do for them. This was no exception for the Tibetan survivors from the Yushu earthquake. Rather than being overwhelmed by sorrow or concern regarding their own future, their priority was to

15

find the corpses of the dead and to bring about favorable rebirth. Unlike the living, who still have the chance to prepare themselves for the final moment, if the dead missed the chance in the intermediate state after death, they would once again wander in samsaric existence.

Big or small, changes are numerous in this fleeting life. We painfully face every death of our loved ones and ultimately our own death. If we can keep the Buddha's teachings in mind and put them into practice, life may become easier for us.

Cause and Effect

Every phenomenon is the result of causes and effects. Within our limited intellectual scope, we can only see a very small part of this causal chain. So we tend to doubt the karmic law of cause and effect when the specific causes and effects across time or space are beyond what we can fathom. Even advanced practitioners cannot explain the totality of causal relationships behind a single phenomenon.

The Buddha had a disciple named Suddhipanthaka. When he first requested ordination from the Buddha, he was refused by the Buddha's other disciples who were arhats and had mastered supernatural clairvoyance. When the Buddha asked them the reason for their rejection, they replied that Suddhipanthaka, in his past five hundred lifetimes, had not made any connection with the Buddha. The Buddha then said, "You are only able to see the causes and conditions within his past five hundred lifetimes, but not earlier when he was a dog and made an inadvertent offering to me. This created a connection between us and served as the reason why he wants to become a monk and to follow me in this life."

The continent of Jambudvipa—the world where we humans live according to Buddhist cosmology—is a place where the force of karma is demonstrated and felt more strikingly. Most people are brought here by their past karma, so their present lives are under the influence of actions undertaken not only in this life but also in past lives, some of which can be traced back several lifetimes or even a few hundred lifetimes. However long the span of time is, these causes will not disappear by themselves. Taking the example of negative actions, there are two main ways to cancel them: to cultivate virtues and to repent and purify karmic obstacles or to do nothing but wait passively until related causes and conditions work together to produce an effect that would naturally exhaust them.

It is said that during the lifetime of the Buddha, the armies of Virudhaka, king of Shravasti, attacked the city of the Shakyas and massacred people there. Of all the Buddha's *shravaka* disciples, Maudgalyayana possessed the greatest miraculous powers. So he rescued five hundred Shakyas in his alms bowl made of iron and raised it high up in the air, hoping to give them refuge, only to find out later that all had died inside regardless.

At that moment, the Buddha himself had a headache. When his disciples asked him why this happened, he replied:

Many lifetimes ago, those Shakyas were fishermen who lived by killing and eating many fish. One day they caught two big ones, and instead of killing them immediately, they left them tied to a pole. As those two fish stranded out of the water writhed in agony, they thought, "These men are killing us even though we have done them no harm. In return, may the day come when we kill them without them having done us any harm." The effect of the two big fishes' thought was that they were reborn as King Virudhaka and his minister Matropakara, while all the other fish killed by the fishermen became their troops. Today, they have massacred the Shakyas. At that time, I myself was the child of one of those fishermen, and watching those two tied-up fish writhing in unbearable agony as they dried, I laughed. The effect of that action is that today I have a headache. But had I not achieved the qualities I now possess, I, too, would have been killed by the troops of Virudhaka.

Apparently, once an effect ripens, nothing can change it. Indeed, how could this not be so for ordinary people, when even the Buddha, who had rid himself of all karmic and emotional obscurations, still had to accept the effect of past actions? We seem to live in a random world of inconceivable coincidences and unexplainable impulses. But the truth is that our fate is pulled and propelled by our own karmic force. We generate causes and in turn bear their effects—good or bad—without exception.

Karma is a Sanskrit word meaning action, and it connotes dynamic force: an action leads to its effect, which brings forth a new action. In this way, causes and effects form a continuum with potent energy, where new elements join ceaselessly. Although the overall trend of this continuum is hard to alter, new actions can either reinforce or weaken the karmic force within. For example, if someone practices Dharma, the effect of his past negative actions, which may lead to his future rebirth in lower realms, may manifest itself as severe pain in his present life. Meanwhile, if he stays positive while enduring the painful effects of negative karma, he adds positive elements to new causes and effects.

If new causes are powerful enough, it is likely that they may even reverse the potential karmic trend, as in the case of Milarepa. Having committed serious wrongs that could have easily cast him into hells, Milarepa practiced Dharma with unimaginable determination and fortitude. Instead of falling into a hell realm, he rose to attain Buddhahood in a single lifetime.

When we see people suffering or dying because of disasters, we should neither regard what happened as accidental without underlying causes, nor think that it is their own fault. Among these people, some may be manifestations of buddhas and bodhisattvas who intend to teach us impermanence, selflessness, and compassion. Some may have successfully canceled the more severe effects through cultivating virtues and practicing Dharma. And some may have finished what needs to be done in this world and be ready to move on to other places.

Our world is filled with intricacy and possibility. In search of the truth, we should be both humble and enthusiastic.

Coexistence

Why do natural disasters occur? We ask this question not because we want to find someone to blame in particular. We ask it because we have concerns about the common future of all beings on this planet, and we are willing to reflect on the role of human activity in shaping this future.

For centuries, our planet has been plagued by natural and human-made problems. Every single day there is news about natural disasters, wars, conflicts, robberies, rapes, fraud, and so on. Every single day there are people dying and suffering. However, we usually do not realize the full gravity of such disasters until one hits close to home. This is precisely where the root of the problem lies: we tend only to care about ourselves and the very few people and things around us. Anything outside our own small box is just a piece of distant news. Yes, there are disasters and people suffering and dying out there, but we are not supposed to be responsible for them. Besides, what can we do about it?

The sense of disconnectedness from the world, or the belief that we are separate from some external reality, is a delusion that erodes our responsibility to others. Modern life increasingly relies on machinery and the service industry. As a result, a phone call to a service company can quickly fix a problem that would have required the effort of a whole family in a previous age. Consequently, our living is made more convenient and independent, but our connections and communications with others become much more limited. And some people even believe that happiness is a private matter—with concern about only what they themselves want and can get, with little regard for the well-being of others.

On the other hand, interdependence among people has increased in modern society, and is greater than in self-sufficient agricultural communities. All our living necessities including food, clothing, shelter, and transportation rely on other people's work. Urbanization also leads to increasing population density. Whether we are at work or at home, we often have to share with others an ever smaller space. Consequently, our actions and speech have greater impact on ourselves and those around us. Living in harmony is not just an aspiration, it is also a necessity for our mutual survival and further advancement.

Such is the paradox of modern society. On the one hand, people are increasingly dependent on one another. Actions taken by a small group of people on one part of the earth will have a greater impact on those living on another part. Yet people perceive themselves as being independent enough to avoid relying on others and to neglect others' well-being.

We all desire happiness and there is nothing wrong with that. But in pursuing it, we need to have consideration for others, including those who live today, those of future generations, and animals, too. People in affluent societies in particular should be more thoughtful about the welfare of others, as the richer and more capable have more resources to help. Although all of us will eventually suffer in one way or another if our living environment deteriorates, the poor and weak are usually affected more deeply than others. It also takes them much longer to get out of trouble and to recover.

Good examples are environmental issues caused by human activity such as the excessive exploitation of natural resources, urban development, water and air pollution, wildlife poaching, and so on. Global warming, climate change, and natural disasters have become regular newspaper headlines and are affecting everybody living on the planet. But for those with limited financial resources in the poorer nations, the chance for survival is much bleaker in the face of disaster, and their difficulties are often exacerbated by especially fragile ecosystems and poor infrastructure.

We used to think of natural disasters and human-made calamities as two separate issues. Gradually, however, we have come to realize that the line between the two is not so clear. Every phenomenon is the product of the interplay of varied causes and effects. One does not have to be an advanced practitioner of Buddhism to understand that our mental activities influence the outer world. That is, our thoughts guide our actions, and our actions in turn affect the external environment within which we live.

Natural disasters do not happen overnight, nor are they driven by a single cause. When they happen, the final trigger often appears to be natural forces. But just as the straw that breaks the camel's back does not represent the whole burden, behind these disasters we find the imprints of human activity. Sociologists have done extensive research on the relationship between human activity and social and environmental development. They certainly have far better knowledge than I do in this field. What I share here is only my personal observations from a layperson's perspective.

What also strikes me is that improving living conditions fails to ease people's physical and mental suffering. It is true that many infectious diseases caused by, for example, poor hygiene have been eradicated or are being controlled, but a succession of new health problems have emerged, such as high blood sugar, gout, and obesity. In developed nations, stress results in an increasing number of people suffering from insomnia and depression, and induces other problems like cardiovascular diseases and cancer.

I am not saying that material advances per se are increasing human suffering. It would be naïve to think that the abandonment of material development would solve every modern problem, for this does not address the root cause we are confronting. Even if we returned to more primitive technologies, we would not necessarily become happier. Yet many of us go to the other extreme, believing that technological advances and material affluence could tackle all problems and eliminate suffering in our times. This is why people compete aggressively for resources. Undoubtedly, material things can bring satisfaction, but only to the physical aspect of our lives. However, it is our need for not only physical pleasures but also spiritual fulfillment that makes us humans unique and distinct from animals.

In addition to material things, people also try to acquire more intellectual resources. Higher education and intellectual credentials are often associated with personal success. Knowing little does not necessarily lead to happiness, but knowledge in itself is not a promise for happiness either. In fact, many people keep themselves updated every day through constant phone calls, a continuous flow of emails, and a vast amount of information. Still they remain anxious and worried that society might marginalize them if they miss something.

Some problems in today's world can indeed be solved—like the eradication of poverty and illiteracy. Yet in many circumstances we still suffer. The deeper cause of human suffering, in my view, lies in our longtime negligence of spiritual development. True and lasting happiness cannot be achieved through external things. If we continue to ignore spiritual development, our problems will remain as they are.

Self-Discipline

My idea of spiritual development has nothing to do with mystical experience or supernatural power. Rather, it is about the cultivation of mental qualities that bring happiness to others and oneself, such as compassion, tolerance, humility, and kindness. In other words, we must care for the welfare of other beings and transform our behaviors accordingly. Thus, spiritual practice entails two indispensable aspects: be thoughtful of others and take relevant actions to transform our own minds.

22

We are born with the ability to feel empathy with other people's joy, anger, and sorrow, as if we experience those emotions ourselves. Seeing someone else suffering induces a sense of sympathy in us, even though not all of us will express compassion and take action to help. Many people, when seeing a news broadcast of a catastrophe, will shed tears and feel an urge to help. The shock and devastation they feel are precisely what people in the disaster area feel. At that moment, one does not have to be a Buddhist to understand the nature of compassion. And if someone is apathetic, it is not because of their inability to be sympathetic. It is very likely that, feeling uneasy, they will either close their eyes or look away if they see the tragic scene. Unable to bear the sight of another being's suffering is another version of sympathy. To further share the suffering of another being is compassion, an ability that is always with us even if we appear to be cold and selfish.

So, what can we do when calamity strikes? Although not all of us can be involved directly in rescue and aid work, I think we can at least share the emotional pains of those affected by giving them a sense of being loved, cared for, and not left alone. One way of sharing, for instance, is to perform transference rituals for the dead, through which we share their fears and loneliness by accompanying them in the intermediate states, and help them to avoid obstacles and obtain a positive rebirth.

Imagine what we may need if we encounter a catastrophe. First, we will need food, clothing, shelter, and so on. Of equal importance is our need for the love and care of others, which is both biologically and emotionally driven. From birth to adulthood, our survival, our growth, and our healthy living rely on love and care. We are born to appreciate the beauty of others' loving-kindness. Any friendly expression, even if as tiny as a sincere smile from a stranger, can touch our heart and bring us joy. Others are just like us, and it is for this reason that we should do our best to help those affected by disasters, understanding their situations and sharing in their suffering.

In the long run, we should not only help those in need but also apply self-discipline if other people's happiness truly matters to us. We should regularly examine our actions in everyday life to refrain from those behaviors that may bring harm to others and ourselves. Doing so will help reduce conflicts among people and groups as well as between humans and nature, making the world more livable and harmonious for all beings. Only when the living environment as a whole becomes more harmonious can there be more equal opportunities for development and better living. This is particularly important for the poor and the weak, including those in disaster zones.

Generally speaking, our mind dictates our actions. If we are able to tame negative emotions and thoughts, our behaviors will be transformed accordingly. Negative emotions refer to mental activities that cause us and others to suffer. For example, anger, hatred, jealousy, anxiety, depression, and fear count as negative emotions. Here I purposely do not use the usual Buddhist term *affliction*, as it entails a broader meaning that involves all actions undertaken by unenlightened beings. More importantly, whenever we talk about the "five poisons" (greed, anger, ignorance, pride, and doubt) or the "three poisons" (greed, anger, ignorance) or other afflictions, I hope we regard them only as emotional experiences and not as the nature of our mind.

Whenever we use the word *affliction*, many of us may have a tendency to associate it with the nature of the mind and think it is afflictive in essence. However, if we say "emotions," it is quite clear that they are not innate and are changeable. Some of them arise frequently, have strong energy, and are difficult to control. Still, they do not reflect the nature of the mind. If anger, for instance, were the nature of the mind, we could never rejoice even for an instant. The truth is that we can be happy, and, at the same time, recognize anger when being angry. This tells us that consciousness and emotions are not necessarily the same. It is possible for us to subdue negative emotions consciously.

Thus, to be mindful is the first step on the path to self-discipline. Being vigilant in our actions of body, speech, and mind, we observe how negative emotions develop and where their destructiveness and deception lie. Even a negative emotion as frantic as fury must go through a gradual process to emerge and is dependent on various conditions to arise and grow. If we understand this process, we can find a way to curb, weaken, and defuse fury. We all have some negative traits. To be mindful and vigilant when they arise should be the core practice of our lives.

However, most people do not make earnest efforts to control negative emotions. Since negative emotions subside by themselves, many think there is no need to counteract them proactively—they believe we should leave them uncontrolled. In general, these people lack an understanding of the destructive nature of negative emotions. They engulf us and paralyze our sense and sensibility. In such a situation, we are unlikely to make sensible decisions and act wisely. Instead, our own interests and those of others will be harmed, and we may even put others and ourselves in danger.

One characteristic of negative emotions is that, if you do not consciously tame them, they will grow stronger each time they arise, and by driving out other emotions, they will eventually dominate your emotional world. You will get used to resorting to one or two negative emotions as you react to everything you encounter. In the case of someone who gets upset easily, that person can always find reasons to get angry even on a happy occasion. We tend to equate that person's mood with their mind, but the truth is that their habitual mood is only the result of their inability to control their anger each time it arises. Their innate mind is by no means an angry mind.

Negative emotions destroy one's peace of mind and their effects can be either short-lived or enduring. The more lasting ones are often induced by our own attitude toward them. When we are in danger, for instance, fear may keep us alert and agile, enabling us to act more efficiently than usual. In this case, fear is not so harmful to our body and mind, and it can sometimes even be helpful. However, if we cling to the sense of fear and obsessively wallow in it, we will only end up even more fearful and fall victim to our own mental intemperance.

The same applies to other negative emotions like hatred, sorrow, and anxiety. As common wisdom goes, one should think positively. Positive thinking does not entail willful oblivion or mental minimizing of unpleasant experiences and emotions. Not dwelling on negative thoughts is a central feature of Buddhist self-discipline.

Our experience tells us that emotions, both negative and positive, are contagious. When someone is in a bad mood, they will affect people around them. Initially, those people may feel irritated. Then they may unwittingly become ill-tempered as well. Slowly and subtly, an unhappy atmosphere dawns and surrounds people in the same circle—a family, a work place, or even a social community. People are, by nature, friendly, honest, and decent. But under the influence of a bad mood, they become upset, aggressive, unforgiving, and sometimes even dishonorable. When most people behave in this way, tension, distrust, and selfishness take root, and happiness becomes out of reach for both individuals and society.

Negative emotions are also deceptive. They give us the illusion that they can protect us and satisfy our needs. Very often we allow ourselves to be angry because we believe it makes us stronger. This can be seen in a debate, where the ones who become impatient and engage in verbal abuse are usually the ones poised to lose. Likewise, arrogance, another negative emotion, reveals one's immaturity and weakness.

Of all the negative emotions, nothing is more deceptive than greed. Very often we believe the seed of our unhappiness is not getting what we want or having too little. The borderline between necessity and luxury is both blurry and subjective. We should be careful not to fall prey to greed and avoid placing too much emphasis on acquiring possessions or status. Take the example of food, which we must eat to live. Though we need food, we can easily overindulge and eat too much, which turns out to be harmful.

Observing our negative emotions carefully, we will find that their existence directly leads to the loss of our happiness. Therefore, self-discipline is essential to both individual and societal happiness. On the other hand, self-discipline does not mean emotional suppression. It does not require one to follow a set of rules. One should not behave pretentiously either. The idea of self-discipline is to have regard for others and to avoid causing them harm. This is why we Buddhists emphasize kind actions and the precepts in the form of laypeople's vows or monastic vows.

Compassion

While happiness comes from inner peace, refraining from negative emotions alone is not enough to develop a resilient and peaceful mind. We also need to cultivate positive mentalities and emotions.

As mentioned, after the earthquake in Yushu, people offered generous help to the victims and worked together with them. In fact, what they fought against was not just the earthquake and its aftermath; they were also trying to overcome the negative emotional fallout. They were not simply building physical homes, but also a safe haven for spiritual practice. Natural disasters bring tremendous suffering, but humanity and its loving-kindness and compassion can heal people's emotional scars. Even one sympathetic thought can help purify the mind and improve one's attitude.

Inside all of us dwells loving-kindness. The key is to know how to activate and develop this quality that brings happiness to others as well as ourselves. One effective way to achieve this is through giving. As the saying goes, giving is like offering roses to others: even if the flowers are gone, their scent lingers. Indeed, both the taker and the giver benefit from the action of giving. The receiver is helped; the giver reaps joy and self-esteem.

There are many ways of giving, one of which is the giving of material things like the donation of goods and money to disaster areas. In fact, this kind of giving can be done by all of us. We can help the financially needy or help those children who cannot otherwise afford basic education. One does not have to be rich to give, since motivation matters more than how much we can offer.

Giving is not for show either, so there is no need to label it charity. You can walk a little farther to buy bread just to support a local general store, or hire a cleaning lady so that she can earn some extra money to support her family. Many people struggle to make ends meet, but not all of them are willing to accept charitable favors. Therefore, to give others an opportunity to support themselves is, broadly speaking, a way of giving, too.

Apart from material things, we can also give time and energy to people who need help. Many people work as volunteers in disaster areas, taking care of the injured and helping with other matters. In normal circumstances, our society also needs similar volunteer services, such as helping orphaned children, people with disabilities, or those who are elderly, lonely, or homeless. The problems our world faces are not only poverty and hunger but also loneliness and apathy.

Another kind of giving is the giving of the Dharma. It refers to any action taken to benefit people through the teaching of Buddhadharma. Accordingly, the giving of the Dharma also includes teaching others to be kind, inspiring and encouraging people who are experiencing difficulties, and helping people to be more loving, positive, and responsible.

Through giving, we no longer cling to things so tightly. Nor are we so self-centered. To our amazement, giving actually brings us a sense of abundance rather than depletion. Since the idea of giving is to learn how to let go of our attachment to a self in order to help others more effectively, it is important for us to have an altruistic motivation. If we are motivated by the drive to compete or show off, the act of giving will reinforce our attachment. And the joy and self-esteem we get from giving will be limited as well.

Many of us feel what we have and do is never good enough. This kind of sentiment gives us a strong sense of deficiency, and it is particularly prevalent in big cities, where people are beset by anxiety and discontent. While the underlying reason may be complex, I believe some seemingly simple solutions can help. Learning to appreciate ourselves is one way. When we are down, we should think that we are not the only ones who are miserable, and that we still have much to be grateful for. Thinking a bit more about our blessings can help lighten our mood. Optimism and contentment are the two important mental qualities that we need to cultivate. They make us feel grounded and positive in a living environment filled with pressure, choices, and temptations. Mental adjustment has never been easy. But we should make an effort because it is necessary for the happiness of all.

Sometimes, our misery is imaginary and the actual circumstances are far less discouraging. However, it is necessary to learn forbearance even if faced with daunting challenges. That is, we should not be fearful but patient and courageous, and stay kind and compassionate to people around us, including those who may hurt us.

Forbearance is often associated with willpower. Certainly, strong willpower can help us to endure tough times, but this is not the quality I am talking about. The forbearance I refer to is our ability to graciously accept whatever comes, for people who do this understand the dependent nature of all things and believe in the karmic law of cause and effect. Forbearance has nothing to do with cowardice either, as its courage arises from our inner resilience and openness to all circumstances. In times of adversity, it is best to keep a gentle and warm heart, remaining kind even in the harshest moments.

There was a girl who had been buried under the rubble for more than ten hours after the Yushu earthquake. The moment she was pulled out, she said to the rescue team, "Sorry to have bothered you.

I'll never forget your kindness in my life." Many people were deeply touched by her words. But some also said that perhaps this was not really what she meant, as her Mandarin was poor and she failed to express herself properly at that emotional moment. Perhaps she did not use precisely the right words, but her message was clear: she was sorry for having bothered people! At the very moment she was saved, she did not think about her own misery but instead humbly expressed her gratitude.

Thanks to forbearance, we will not fall into the trap of negative emotions but stay sanguine and sensible. It allows us to take proper and peaceful measures to solve problems and avoid further harm. It also makes us tolerant, rational, and amicable. In this regard, forbearance means tolerance—to accept the diversity of the world. Most of us only want to change others but not ourselves. It is therefore not so easy to be tolerant.

Mental transformation is not easy either. Our habits have been developed over a very long period of time and are impossible to change in a short period. To overcome difficulties and setbacks on our path, we must have forbearance and patience. Meanwhile, always remember that our ultimate goal in life is to help all sentient beings to attain happiness and freedom from suffering. By our loving-kindness and positive actions, may we build a pure and joyful heaven on earth.

This Precious Human Existence

It was late 2009 when I started to suffer from angina and slept poorly most nights. While I suspected it might have been caused by heart disease, I did not manage to see a cardiologist for two months. The result, unfortunately, was most worrisome.

Having heard the news, many of my students pledged to do virtuous acts as a way to pray for my recovery. Among them, some would save millions of animal lives; some would make thousands of light offerings; some would recite one million times or even ten million times the one-hundred-syllable mantra. One student told me that the coming Chinese New Year would be the most meaningful one in his life because he would save animals from slaughter or captivity for five consecutive days during the New Year festivities. In light of these promises and kind acts, I was thankful that my illness at the turn of the year had some positive impact on others.

Being sick is a part of life. For most of us, it entails suffering for those who are ill and apprehension for those around them. Other than that, there is no positive meaning behind it. Yet if we can interpret sickness as an opportunity and see what lessons we can draw from it, it can be a good chance for us to cultivate renunciation and bodhichitta, the awakening mind.

The Buddha teaches us that spiritual liberation starts with one's understanding of suffering. And the agony of illness is likely to make us understand suffering better. There are many causes and conditions in everyday life that induce disillusionment, unhappiness, and afflictions. Most of our days are spent either worrying or being ill. Yet we choose to ignore the obvious and not talk about

31

it; after all, suffering is an unpleasant topic. When in trouble, our usual reaction is to escape or pretend that nothing has happened. But if illnesses, especially serious ones, befall us, we have nowhere to escape to. In this situation, we might be more willing to look at our experience and reflect on the meaning of suffering, and in a larger sense, the meaning of life itself.

Birth, Old Age, Sickness, and Death

In Buddhism, suffering is divided into three categories, from the gross to the subtle: the suffering of suffering, the suffering of change, and the all-pervasive suffering of conditioning.

The suffering of suffering refers to that which is explicitly unpleasant and undesirable, such as physical pain, mental agony, sickness, fear, separation, and death. Nobody will mistake it for happiness, and all wish to be free from it.

The suffering of change refers to experiences and things that are usually regarded as bringing happiness but that over time lead to suffering. This is because these experiences or things are, ultimaitely, suffering by nature. For instance, eating is necessary for us to live, and good food pleases us, but many health problems are caused by what we eat. If food by nature is happiness, then the more we eat, the happier we become. However, our level of sensory pleasure does not necessarily increase with higher food consumption—overeating makes us feel uncomfortable or even sick. Evidently, the pleasure of eating carries elements of suffering. Likewise, other unhealthy activities, such as excessive TV watching or late-night partying or drinking, are thought to bring pleasure but actually cause potential health problems.

In fact, everything that appears to represent life's happiness carries the seed of future suffering, but it is difficult to see this without careful examination. Meeting with friends is fun until everyone inevitably departs. An intimate relationship, however sweet and romantic, comes with arguments, doubts, and frustrations, not to mention potential separation. Youth and beauty gradually yield to the passing of time, and the ugliness of aging eventually surfaces. Parenthood is joyful, but the responsibility to raise a little, fragile life is tedious and tiresome. Career promotion gives one a sense of achievement, but pressure and anxiety are its price. And to be fabulously rich entails the burden of preserving and distributing wealth.

Relative to the previous two, the third type of suffering—the all-pervasive suffering of conditioning—is much subtler and more profound. It refers to the basic state of helplessness and imperfection pervading all forms of life in cyclic existence. Our various existences are propelled by karmic forces and consequently entail endless afflictions, and our afflictive minds drive us to be reborn again and again in the ocean of suffering, unable to control our destiny.

To be more specific, we humans suffer from eight kinds of suffering. Rich or poor, strong or weak, we all have to suffer from the pain of birth, old age, sickness, and death. In addition, we may also have to suffer the dread of meeting hated enemies or losing loved ones, as well as the pain of not getting what we want or encountering what we seek to avoid.

Let us take a look at sickness. Regular exercise and a healthy lifestyle can prevent certain diseases. However meticulously we look after our health, though, it is impossible for us not to get sick over the course of our lives. If we fall ill, we must take medicine, or perhaps even be bedridden, unable to do and eat as we wish. If we get seriously ill, we may be hospitalized and have to go through a long and painful treatment. The incessant struggle with illness and pain can sometimes even make us feel worse than dying.

Another inevitable form of suffering is aging. If we are fortunate enough not to have died at a young age, we will eventually meet the uncomfortable realities of aging such as thin hair, deep wrinkles, false teeth, and weak eyesight. Our memory fades and gradually we cannot recognize people around us. These can drive people away at the time we need them most, and loneliness becomes our only companion. Death will ultimately separate us from our loved ones as well as those things dear to us. Yet we would rather welcome its early arrival, as if it were a lasting relief from the unbearable agony of solitude.

Such talk about the pervasiveness of suffering may appear pessimistic, but this is not my intention at all. If we only perceive suffering as negative, we will certainly try to elude it. Or we may regard it as a sign of failure that can easily be avoided with competence and tactics. If this is our general outlook, we will undoubtedly feel frustrated and anxious when encountering difficulties and setbacks. We may regard ourselves as the most unfortunate yet innocent people in the world: "Why always me!" "Why do I have to suffer so much?" We may also look for others to blame: "It's all because of him. If he had not done that, I would not be in trouble." Doing so perhaps helps relieve our anxiety and fear temporarily, but our problem remains unsolved.

Sometimes, evasion may make us more anxious and fearful. Without tolerance and patience for suffering, we become vulnerable in difficult circumstances. Life in turn becomes bleaker than it should be. However, if we change our mentality and accept the fact that suffering is an inherent part of life, we will be able to focus on solving the problems themselves rather than dwelling on negative emotions. The latter only increases our sense of frustration and grievance without offering any constructive solution.

In order to minimize or eliminate suffering, our seeing of its pervasiveness must be followed by further insight into it. It is like dealing with disease. Once we have adequate medical knowledge, we can adjust our habits and lifestyle to prevent it or to at least minimize its consequences. Otherwise, we might be caught unprepared, not knowing how to react or even losing hope. Actually, it is possible for us to be calm and graceful when facing disease and other kinds of suffering.

In some cases, our familiarity with suffering helps us deal directly with its causes and guard against it. In other cases, we are unable to influence the consequences once the causes and conditions have come together, leaving no room for remedy. If so, it would be wise to prepare ourselves for the inevitable pain, as this enables us to be less susceptible to unnecessary emotional agonies like fear and anxiety in addition to what we already have to endure.

Shantideva once said, "If there is a solution to the problem, you do not need to worry; if there is no solution, worrying is useless anyway." We can try to apply this teaching to illness. Medical research shows that positive attitudes are beneficial for recovery, whereas negative emotions like anger are harmful.

Suffering is ubiquitous, and life can never be perfect. If we understand this deeply, we can begin to relax. No longer will we try to escape, blame, or even reverse our circumstances when troubles occur. We start to understand that as long as we live, we cannot avoid old age, sickness, and death, and that as long as we have greed, anger, ignorance, and pride, emotional afflictions will always be with us.

Where Do We Find a Self?

It would be quite foolish, nonetheless, if we were to lose hope and optimism in the face of unavoidable suffering. The purpose of observing and reflecting on all-pervasive suffering is that we have the potential to be freed from it. It is for this reason that the Buddha, through his teaching on the truth of suffering, guides us to see suffering as being the very nature of samsara. The more insights we gain into it, the more inspired we will be to explore its root causes and antidotes.

Suffering and happiness do not come without their causes. The Buddha says that the cause of all suffering originates from our deep-rooted misperception of both self and the world. Perceiving the illusory as real, we fail to see the universal truth that all phenomena come and go depending on necessary internal and external causes and conditions. They are not inherently substantial and permanent. In Buddhism, we call such characteristics selflessness and impermanence.

Impermanence was not something invented by the Buddha. Rather, the Buddha stated an obvious truth to which most of us remain oblivious. Flowers bloom and wilt. Seasons alternate. The moon waxes and wanes. Joy and sorrow take turns. Time flows constantly with each passing moment and nothing stays forever. Such is impermanence, the rhythm of our universe. Despite its omnipresence, we do not take notice of impermanence until unexpected or even drastic changes occur. Consequently, we misperceive impermanence as the maker of life's misery, not knowing that our own fear of change is the real culprit.

To overcome such fear, we can either become familiar with impermanence or gain insight into the cause of the fear. Most of us know that the more we shun the things we fear, the more fearful we become of them. Our relationship with impermanence is quite similar. If we turn around and look straight at impermanence, we may find it not as scary as imagined. Without impermanence, for instance, night would always prevail, those separated would never reunite, an unhealthy body would remain sick, and the depressed would never rejoice. Wouldn't it be dreadful if our world were like this?

Observing changes in our lives and our environment can cultivate our insight into impermanence and enable us to accept it. We will no longer be obsessed with getting rid of wrinkles, be overly self-conscious about our saggy stomachs, feel heartbroken after parting ways with someone, or be frustrated by failures. We will begin to approach life's unexpected turns more wisely and practically. If we get old, suffer sickness, encounter setbacks, or feel insecure, we know that we are not alone. Changes pervade every aspect of life and affect every single person. Every one of us has ups and downs, and we gain things and lose things from time to time. It is a reality that is both universal and natural.

Insight into impermanence not only makes us more open-minded but also more appreciative of our lives, allowing us to see the value of spiritual practice. Quite often, people like to talk about how short this life is. But deep down, they think that they will always have enough time to do what they plan to do. Consequently, even big changes in their lives, like severe illness or the death of relatives, are unlikely to alter their habitual blindness to impermanence, let alone the misfortunes of others. Those who gather for a party might carry on despite hearing the news of an earthquake. Those who have suffered from health problems will rarely see, after recovery, the senselessness of chasing fame and wealth within their limited lifespans. Compared to fame and wealth, inner peace, contentment, loving-kindness, and compassion are more beneficial to their lives and more easily make them happy.

People easily become sad and desperate when misfortunes befall them. Yet they are forgetful and eventually return to their old ways, failing to learn the lessons from their suffering. I am not saying that it is wrong to be optimistic. But while being optimistic, we should also see the fragile and fleeting nature of life. Aging and death come closer every day. The time we can use to cultivate virtue and wisdom is limited. Yet we spend our lives on trivialities, clinging to things that do not last. Sometimes, we even act immorally to achieve our desires.

When life comes to its end, nothing helps but the Dharma. At death, we cannot take a single coin with us even if we are wealthy, or a single servant even if our power matches that of a king. Instead, we must leave everything behind, including our cherished body. On the other hand, no one and nothing can harm us but our own negative actions done in the past, even if the whole world is our enemy.

Further, impermanence is not to our liking because of the intimidating message it entails: all things including ourselves are selfless in nature, lacking intrinsic existence, concreteness, and permanence. They are only the products of causes and conditions, the physical and nonphysical elements necessary for various phenomena to emerge. For a phenomenon to arise, certain causes and conditions must come together. Otherwise, there will be no phenomenon. For the same reason, if these causes and conditions change, the phenomenon changes accordingly; if they cease, the phenomenon ceases as well. This view is called "dependent arising" in Buddhism. Since all phenomena originate dependently, they do not exist permanently and there is no inherent and completely independent self in them. This gives rise to selflessness, another Buddhist concept.

Like impermanence, selflessness is a mere reflection of universal reality and is neither good nor bad. It may not be particularly appealing when we first hear of it, for it can shatter our illusion of security and make us feel disheartened. We have believed for a long time that things exist in a truly independent way, and this mode of existence is what makes life meaningful and happy. Consequently, we are more inclined to resist the idea of selflessness being the essence of all things including ourselves.

It is indeed not easy to comprehend selflessness, let alone to experience and realize it. Everything around us—including ourselves—appear existent like solid rocks. We all have individual bodies and thoughts; I am not you and you are not me. We can see and touch those tables and walls and water. How can they be selfless?

The concept of selflessness has been elaborated on by two great Buddhist masters: Nagarjuna in his *Fundamental Verses of the Middle Way* and Shantideva in his "On Wisdom," the last chapter of *The Way of the Bodhisattva*. I will only provide a brief introduction here by using examples from our daily experiences.

Based on analysis alone, we can easily demonstrate that the idea of intrinsic existence is both illusory and misleading. For example, we use the concepts of "I" and "myself" as reference points to communicate with others, but the truth is that we are unable to identify a concrete and substantial self. If the physical body is this self, does losing weight mean this self is diminished and "I" am no longer "I"? And if so, where is the other part of the self supposed to go? Nobody would think like this. After losing weight, we do not doubt our individual identity, and we will even believe that our self has improved. If we perceive ourselves as the same person regardless of changes in our physical shape, this self must be changeable. A changeable thing will not last, and it transforms constantly with external and internal changes. This leaves no room for an intrinsic and concrete "I." Thus the perception of the physical body as a stable "I" is only a delusion.

Likewise, none of the various parts of the body is an"I." If blood or body fluids count as the"I," am "I" not getting smaller every time "I" sweat or cry? Do "I" become another person after "I" receive a blood transfusion from somebody else? The fact that the same blood can run in both my veins and the veins of another proves that blood itself is by no means an independent "I." The same analysis can be applied to all the four elements of earth, water, fire, and air that constitute the physical body. And we will arrive at the same conclusion that none of these can ground a self-subsistent "I."

There are other ways to reach the conclusion as well. Just look at our photos as a toddler. Is that giggling, toothless child held in the arms of an adult really me? If so, where has that "I" gone, and who is the person looking at the photo at this very moment?

Our human body, formed by physical aggregates that undergo gradual but constant changes, may last years, decades, or even a hundred years. By way of contrast, our thoughts, emotions, and feelings constituting consciousness that arise and disperse instantly are much less enduring. If the relatively stable physical body is not "I," it is even less likely for this consciousness to be one.

When we speak of selflessness, it is important to note that we do not mean nihilism. Life is the interplay of incessant and interwoven changes. Neither the same nor different, neither inconsistent nor abiding, the present "I" and the previous "I" are connected through interrelated causes and effects. A previous physical or mental activity influences and produces the current one that, dependently originated, produces in turn the next one. This causal chain of dependent arising is what drives the infinite but ever-changing flow of life. Death is nothing more than one of life's most profound changes. And it will not stop the coming and going of causes and effects.

Not only "I" but also all the things around us are examples of selflessness. Scientific progress makes it easier to comprehend. We now know that every material substance that can be seen, touched, and felt is made of atoms, which are held together by chemical bonds to form molecules. Every atom is composed of protons, neutrons, and electrons. These small particles bond together in various manners and move constantly at a high speed, and we mistake the trajectories of their movements for objects that exist truly. In a dark night, a burning incense stick can create a light trace if we wave it fast enough. The light trace, after all, is no more than an optical illusion created by the burning stick at various spots. Unfortunately, the same kind of illusion also fools us when phenomena appear.

A human body, if examined under a microscope, will also appear differently. The concrete physical appearance that we usually behold will be replaced with water, gases, minerals, and other substances, which can be reduced further to molecules, atoms, and even smaller particles, if we keep raising the magnification of the instrument. Works by the Middle Way school of Buddhist philosophy founded by Nagarjuna have explained that all phenomena perceived as inherently existent are void-like space, though some other schools of Buddhism hold different views. Scientific studies have shown that an inherent and abiding self does not exist: even if a material substance can ultimately be reduced to the smallest possible particles rather than being void, this kind of particle can still not constitute an intrinsically existent self. Otherwise, there would be numerous selves in every human body, and at the same time, in the air, water, and soil. This brings us back to the starting point. which one is it if there is an intrinsically existent self?

A Snake or a Rope?

We are fortunate to hear this view of selflessness, for it offers us a new vantage point from which to see the world and an effective way to alleviate suffering. However, it is not for intellectual curiosity but for the cessation of suffering that we explore the subject of selflessness. To understand selflessness at the intellectual level alone is not sufficient to reach our goal. The elimination of suffering relies on our ultimate realization of selflessness.

The metaphor of the rope and snake is often used to illustrate the relation between suffering and the realization of selflessness. Entering a dark room, someone mistakes a rope on the floor for a snake and is terrified. If they are told at that moment that what they see is just a rope and not a snake, their fear might abate but not disappear entirely, for they might still have doubts. If they turn on the light and see with their own eyes that it is indeed a rope, they will completely be rid of fear. Likewise, we suffer from samsaric existence because we take dependently arising and transient things as real. Hearing about the Buddha's teaching on selflessness and knowing in theory that the origin of suffering is our attachment to a self, we nevertheless continue to suffer from afflictions. This suffering can only cease when we realize the nature of selflessness.

If we merely regard the view of selflessness as a piece of knowledge and do not put it into practice, it is like reading a doctor's prescription without getting the medicine and taking it when we are ill. In order to bring about inner change and subdue afflictions, we need to apply this teaching to our daily life and experience its meaning through practice.

Beginners are unlikely to experience selflessness directly. It is thus important to cultivate the awareness that all things are selfless. When falling ill, for instance, instead of simply lamenting your condition, tell yourself that there is not a self that is inherently existent but rather an ever-changing aggregate of flesh, bones, veins, blood, and so on; that only a part of this bodily form does not function well; and that the pain and discomfort are only short-lived sensory experiences. By merely acknowledging the absence of an inherently existent self that is suffering from illness, we can already release much of the anxiety and fear.

A student of mine once cut his finger by accident. With a gasp he said to himself, "Phew, that's what attachment to a self is like!" This told me something: whenever experiencing physical or mental pain, I shall just regard it as no more than my attachment to a self rather than take the pain too seriously. Such an attitude enables us to deal with pain more effectively.

Quite often we do the opposite and exaggerate the pain by spinning it into a drama. If someone cuts their finger, they may just need a Band-Aid, yet they sit there and entertain various thoughts: *I am bleeding; I could catch tetanus; tetanus is fatal; and if I die, what will happen to my kids?* If they keep thinking along these lines, they might end up having a heart attack. This may sound hyperbolic, but we are not dissimilar in many situations.

Selflessness also helps us reduce attachment to things. For instance, diamond and graphite are valued differently. But given that they both are allotropes of carbon, they are in fact not so different. It is only the variation in their carbon atoms' bonding that gives them distinct properties in terms of hardness and crystallinity. Diamond is the hardest known natural mineral, while graphite is one of the softest. Diamond is brilliant with high dispersion of light, while graphite is black and looks dull. Being carbon in essence, neither diamond nor graphite has the intrinsic nature of being diamond or graphite. Yet our deluded attachment gives rise to their different values. Diamond is inlaid in crowns and necklaces as a symbol of wealth and extravagance; graphite is ground into powder and mixed with clay just to make pencils. Diamond fashions people's dreams, while graphite is ever out of the limelight. Such is the way we see the world, projecting our deluded thoughts on things that in themselves have no inherent attributes of being ugly or fine, cheap or valuable. Fooled by our delusion, we suffer unnecessarily.

While all phenomena are selfless in nature, they are dependently arising and primarily governed by the karmic law of cause and effect. Someone who knew little about Buddhism once asked me how I would summarize Buddhist belief in just one sentence. I thought for a while and said, "Having faith in Buddhism is to believe in causes and effects." Despite their supremacy, Buddhist notions of selflessness, emptiness, and the like are difficult to comprehend for the average person. If someone mistakes selflessness for nihilism, their views and actions will deviate from the right path and they will miss the prospect of enlightenment. Therefore, I think it is more appropriate for beginners to start with the law of cause and effect, the basic yet essential and most practical and profound part of Buddhism.

In practice, believing in causality means to do positive things and to refrain from negative actions. It is also about clearing away cognitive obscurations and cultivating an unbiased mind. If we want to avoid suffering, we should abandon all thoughts and acts that will cause it. If we want happiness, we should develop thoughts and acts that will bring it.

Some may say, "I'm diligent in Dharma practice. But why do I still encounter hardship and misfortune? Why do those who have done wrong still enjoy a better life? Does the karmic law of cause and effect really work?" New grass grows shortly after the sowing of seeds, but it takes a year for barley to blossom and yield crops. The law of cause and effect works in the same way. Despite the timing difference, every single thought or act eventually leads to an effect. If the effect of a past action is yet to arise and you have not taken any action to prevent it from ripening, it will surely come to fruition sometime in the future. What we experience in the present life is the result not only of this life's actions but also those done in our previous lives. Likewise, some effects of what we do now will only come to fruition in our future lives.

The *Diamond Cutter Sutra* says, "Virtuous men and women that believe, practice, read, and recite this sutra, if disdained by others, would have fallen into the evil realms due to their negative karma in past lives, but due to the disdain of others in the present life the karmic offenses of their former lives will then be lessened, and they will attain supreme perfect enlightenment." These words show that virtuous acts create new causes and conditions, which alter the original causal chain and enable us to mitigate the potentially severe effects of past negative deeds. The ill consequences, which we would have to suffer in future lives, now take the form of less severe pain in this life. This is why, in some cases, we may still suffer from misfortunes despite doing virtuous acts. It is therefore essential to keep karmic law in mind and be cautious with our thoughts and actions in everyday life.

Many years ago, food offerings were made to the monastic members at the Larung Buddhist Institute during a Dharma gathering over several days. To decide how to handle the daily leftovers, His Holiness Jigme Phuntsok Rinpoche called all the khenpos and tulkus at Larung to a meeting. As part of the food offerings to the monastic members, those leftovers still belonged to the monastic community, and not managing them properly would be very wrong. If they were thrown away, it would be both wasteful and inappropriate. If the leftovers were given away to animals or to laypeople, both the givers and the receivers would have to bear the karmic effect of rebirth in hell. We looked to the sutras and tantras for guidance, and after an intense discussion, we reached a solution. During the offering period, the leftover food of the day would be sold and the proceeds would then be used to buy new food to be consumed the next day. This practice would be repeated until no more food from the offerings was left.

His Holiness Jigme Phuntsok Rinpoche once said that sometimes he felt sure of his liberation from samsara and was happy for himself, but sometimes he was not so sure because of his early experience at Nubzur Monastery. When he was a young monk at Nubzur, he was well liked and often received extra food in addition to his regular portions from the stewards. He later thought that this might become an obstacle to obtaining a favorable rebirth. He also felt sorry for the stewards who failed to distribute the monastic food correctly and would have to bear negative karmic consequences. As a result, His Holiness often arranged rituals to be performed at Larung for their early liberation.

Under the influence of His Holiness, I have always been very cautious in dealing with common properties related to the Three Jewels. I seldom, for example, eat and drink in the monasteries where I go to teach or visit. Occasionally, if I have to take meals there, I always insist on paying. According to Buddhist sutras, when it comes to common properties of the Sangha, taking monastic food will cause the most severe effects. If someone steals jewelry and clothing on buddha statues and decides to wear them, the negative karma might be purified if they later repent and return with new clothes and jewelry. However, if a layperson eats the food that belongs to a monastic community, or a monk eats the food of a monastic community beyond what is provided, the negative karma cannot be completely cleansed even if they repent and compensate for it later.

The late Khenpo Pema Wangtse was a student of the eminent Thubga Rinpoche. He once taught at Tashi Monastery, where he emphasized the importance of observing the law of cause and effect by Buddhist practitioners. He himself set a good example as a person cautious regarding deeds. He had no possessions other than a box of books, which he took with him wherever he went. One winter, the monastery held a Dharma ceremony that lasted for several days. During that period, firewood was collected and burned to make teas and porridges for the participating monks. Some of the monks, after the daily ceremony, would then use the remaining unfinished charcoals to warm their private rooms. When Khenpo Pema Wangtse came to fetch the charcoals, he always brought the same amount of unused firewood in exchange. He said, "It goes without saying that one should be cautious with the Sangha's food. But even just a piece of used firewood must be handled with caution if it also belongs to the Sangha."

By the same token, we must be cautious with our words. When I was young, I used to study under the guidance of Khenpo Tsewang Jigme. He often talked about a mistake he regretted deeply. And sometimes when he talked about it in class, tears of remorse would roll down his cheeks.

It was many years ago, when Khenpo Tsewang Jigme studied at the Dzogchen Shri Singha Institute. One day a scholar from the Geluk school of Tibetan Buddhism who was both eloquent and fond of debate arrived from Lhasa's Drepung Monastry. When the revered Khenpo Gherer was teaching the Middle Way, the scholar joined the class, too, but acted disrespectfully to the teacher. Khenpo Gherer was soft spoken and liked to explain subjects at a slow pace. As he was explaining the fundamentals of emptiness, this scholar, who happened to be sitting next to Khenpo Tsewang Jigme, shook his head in disapproval while repeating Khenpo Gherer's words. Displeased at his gesture, Khenpo Tsewang Jigme challenged the scholar to a debate on the *Treasury of Abhidharma* composed by Vasubandhu, one of the greatest Buddhist authorities in ancient India. In the middle of the debate, the scholar made a mistake. And with a sound of triumph, Khenpo pounced on it immediately, "Nonsense, you idiot! Neither Vasubandhu nor his followers have ever said such a thing." Later Khenpo Tsewang Jigme felt so sorry for insulting the scholar that he decided never to debate again.

A Boat, a Bridge, and a Passage for
Those Desiring the Farther Shore

Phenomena arising dependently do not exist on their own or in isolation. This understanding of selflessness helps weaken our dualistic thinking and allows us to see the pain and futility of building an ego-based barrier when interacting with others. It makes it easier to understand and accommodate others, and our relation with the environment becomes more harmonious. It is also this understanding of the interdependence and connections among all things that makes possible the very practice of bodhichitta, the vast attitude of bodhisattvas.

Every time I go to a hospital, I see corridors crowded with people in pain, old and young, sobbing and silent. My heart saddens, and I wish I could do something for them. Illness makes people both vulnerable and sensitive. Any kind gesture will bring comfort to patients or their worried loved ones.

My recent medical examination was arranged by a student and did not require me to wait for very long. Later I learned that the test center I visited can only accommodate around ten patients each day. The waiting list is long and it takes weeks or even months to get an appointment. My heart sank when I heard this since I caused at least one patient to wait an extra day. If that person was very ill, their illness may have gotten worse due to the delay. Maybe they came from another city and had to stay in a guesthouse. If they were also poor, one more day's waiting would add an extra financial burden. Instead of being helpful, I made that person's life more difficult.

We often talk about our aspiration to benefit all sentient beings. Yet the words *sentient beings* can just be empty rhetoric. Afraid of missing the big picture by paying too much attention to individuals, we are often negligent and indifferent to relatives, friends, and people around us who may be suffering greatly. We can easily forget that the term *sentient beings* is not just a collective noun. It actually represents people and animals we meet every day who, despite all their differences, are alive to pain and happiness just like we are. It is true that we Mahayana Buddhists keep in mind the welfare of all sentient beings that are as vast as space. But it is equally important not to ignore the individuals who come to us for help. Their happiness—temporal or lasting, present or future—should always matter to us.

Suffering and its relation to enlightenment is a major subject in Buddhist literature, and many practitioners of the past chose to lead an ascetic life accordingly. However, it does not mean that Buddhists regard suffering as good and desirable. Obviously, all sentient beings want happiness, which, I believe, is the most fundamental drive of life. To remind ourselves regularly of this common pursuit will help us develop empathy and generate bodhichitta.

The great vows of Samantabhadra—the bodhisattva associated with enlightenment actions—says:

> May all sentient beings in the ten directions,
> Be happy and free from afflictions,
> Benefit from profound and truthful Dharma,
> And achieve true and complete cessation of suffering.

This verse captures well the essence of bodhichitta in aspiration. First, we wish all sentient beings to be happy and free of suffering, and secondly we wish that all sentient beings follow the path of liberation to attain complete enlightenment. Whereas we may be ready to renounce worldly concerns for ultimate liberation, people around us may not be. Instead, they want to remove immediate pains and feel happy in the present. So, it is important for us to respect the differences regarding how happiness is defined and achieved, and do our best to help people regardless of their beliefs. This, in fact, is part of bodhichitta.

For a practitioner, being ill is an effective way to develop empathy toward others' pain and their yearning for health and happiness. When we are healthy, we are slow to appreciate the advantages and preciousness of our abilities to hear, sense, smell, taste, and see what surrounds us, and to cry, laugh, run, jump, eat, and sleep whenever we want. And the color of the universe, the twitter of birds, the scent of flowers, the coolness of a breeze, the flavors of various kinds, all seem so utterly common. But when we get sick, our awareness of them begins to transform.

No wonder the gods and goddesses of the divine realms who do not experience suffering are less able to gain liberation. Their lives are so comfortable that they do not have the desire to pursue enlightenment. Only when they are about to die do they see the pain that is approaching, but by then it is too late. Unlike them, our human life is a combination of good and bad, and we intuitively have a strong desire to avoid suffering and look for happiness. With the right guidance, we may further realize that none of the worldly things, such as fame, wealth, health, and longevity, will last. They will eventually all turn into suffering, the pervasive nature of samsara. The only way to eliminate suffering completely is to escape samsara by attaining ultimate liberation.

A Blind Turtle, a Yoke, and
Their Chance Meeting at Sea

Despite all its imperfection, human life, according to the Buddha, is our best chance for liberation: it brings enough suffering to trigger the desire for liberation, but at the same time is not too painful to discourage practice. Everything we experience in life, from birth to death, gathering to parting, rising to falling, is meant to awaken our mind. But unaware of the preciousness of this human life, the vast majority of us spend it on worldly concerns and overlook the messages and opportunities it conveys.

49

How difficult it is to obtain a human rebirth is unknown to us. Imagine the whole cosmos of a billion universes as a vast ocean. Floating on it is a yoke with a hole in it. Tossed around by the waves, this yoke never stays in the same place for an instant. Deep down in the depth of the ocean lives a blind turtle, who rises up to the surface only once every hundred years. The yoke itself is inanimate, with no intention to look for the turtle; the turtle, being blind, is not intentionally seeking the yoke. So, it is extremely unlikely that the two might meet. Nevertheless, by sheer chance the turtle might still just slip its neck into the yoke at the very moment it surfaces. According to Buddhist scriptures, rarer than this occurrence is rebirth as a human—and even rarer is the chance for us to utilize human life for spiritual practice. Being human, we are temporarily free of the suffering and ignorance of the lower realms of existence including the hells and the realms of the hungry ghosts and animals. We are also unlike the gods of the Brhatphala worlds, who spend their time in a state of mental blankness and mistake it for liberation. Even among humans, some are born in remote places where or in a time when Buddhist teachings are unknown; some are unable to learn or practice the Dharma due to mental or physical deficiency; and some live in an environment that does not offer access to Buddhism.

By comparison, we are much more fortunate. After drifting in the sea of samsara for a long time, we finally come to this part of the human world where Buddhism is taught and practiced; we have heard and developed faith in Buddhism thanks to our karmic connections; we have taken refuge in the Three Jewels and met authentic and qualified teachers; and we do not lead a conflicting lifestyle. In Buddhism, we call such a life—complete with its freedoms and advantages conducive to the practice of the Dharma—the precious human life endowed with freedoms and advantages. Used wisely, this present life is the turning point for us to attain liberation.

Observing carefully, we will find that too many people lack the necessary causes and conditions conducive to spiritual practice. Some of us may be smart and capable, but only use the skills to acquire food, clothes, and other material things, or even worse, to perform negative deeds. It is through the power of all the merit we have accumulated in our numerous past lives that we have now obtained this human rebirth. Without the right sense of purpose, it will be wasted on meaningless trifles and can even become a cause for rebirth in the lower realms.

I often have to deal with vendors and butchers in the market in order to save animals. Some of them told me that it is not their wish to be involved in businesses associated with animal killing, selling, or buying. They are either from families that have been involved in the same business for generations, or have little skill to do anything else. I always feel very sorry for them after hearing their stories. There are many ways to earn a living, and many of us have clean and decent jobs. But they have to labor in the foul conditions of the fish, meat, or poultry markets year after year. Knowing that it would be hard to change their circumstances, I often invite them to join our animal life-release so that they can cultivate merit. Like them, many others earn a living by doing negative things, such as hunters, thieves, and sex workers. Thus, we should be thankful for our comfortable living without the need to do any job contrary to the Dharma.

In 2010, some of my relatives were hospitalized. Then, I myself suffered from a serious heart disease. As a result, I had to go to the hospital quite often. The doctors, nurses, and patients I met there eventually became my friends. Most of them did not have faith in Buddhism. It was not that they disagreed with the teachings, but rather that they had had no opportunity to study them. They saw life's impermanence and suffering, but they felt powerless since the path of total liberation was unknown to them.

Having heard their stories, I realized how fortunate I was, born in a land where Buddhism is deep in people's hearts and minds. I developed a strong faith in the law of cause and effect at a very young age; I had confidence in enlightenment, provided I practiced well; and I left home in my teens to study Buddhism under qualified teachers, believing that the best thing I could do in this life was to follow the path of liberation.

For us, this kind of understanding, this kind of conviction, is rather important, especially in the age of materialism when values and common decency can be in short supply. In times like now, it is not easy to be a good person. Too many temptations can cloud and erode one's belief in inner goodness. Virtuous acts can sometimes even bring criticism or defamation. If our goal were not liberation, and if its path were not through the elimination of greed, anger, and ignorance, as well as through the practice of doing positive deeds and avoiding negative ones, we could easily lose our way. We might continue desiring wealth, fame, respect, and praise, in fear of poverty, contempt, criticism, and humiliation.

At one stage of my illness, I felt my days might soon come to an end. Several doctors gathered in the ward to have a case conference with me. When I looked out the window, the bleak wintry scene met my eyes, and the sadness of others entered my thoughts. If I were to die soon, my mother, whose life was already filled with much hardship, would have to suffer the pain of losing her son. My kind and devoted students, whom I am happy to help on the Buddhist path, would be left alone in sorrow. I also thought about things yet to be finished, wishing that I could express all my final thoughts before I died.

In circumstances like this, it was easy to be sentimental, and I was no exception. But quickly my spiritual training made me realize the uselessness of being sentimental. Life can never be perfect. Each of us has our individual karmic conditions and connections. Trying to grasp people and things that will not last is meaningless. At a time when I had to let go of this human body, I should instead be thinking about whether I can turn death into an opportunity for liberation.

My niece, Ghamo, is a Buddhist nun. She was also critically ill and hospitalized at that time. But she appeared exceptionally calm. She said that she grew up in poor health and always worried about her illness being a burden to the family. Ghamo also said that she hoped for a quick death if she could not make a recovery this time, thus not causing prolonged suffering to her family; that although her life might be short, she had observed the precepts well and was not afraid of death; and that she had faith in her teacher and the Three Jewels, who would bless and guide her to a rebirth in the Pure Land.

I admire Ghamo for her composure, which is rare for a young person like her. Never complaining and seemingly content with everything, she does not have the faintest attachment to the temporal world. During her treatment, she changed wards three times. Her unusual gentleness and tranquility touched her roommates so greatly that they all developed faith in Buddhism. Seeing this, I wished I could be like her and many other true practitioners, who stay graceful in the face of death. Unknown to me at that time, this challenge was just around the corner.

The life we are leading is short-lived. Once we lose it, it will be extremely difficult to obtain another human rebirth. Many people assume, for no explicable reason, that cyclic existence is a series of romantic episodes. Not only do they take human rebirth for granted but also think that they can always return to the same dramas and play the same characters. This is wishful thinking indeed. If all people had control over their future, most of them, I trust, would choose not to die. The reality, though, is that most people are actually unable to control their destiny at the time of death.

As the saying goes: to know what you have done in past lives, look at what you are experiencing in this life; to know what will happen in future lives, look at what you are doing in this life. Whether or not we will be reborn as a human depends on what we do now. To take a rebirth in the human or divine realms, we must perform virtuous deeds and avoid actions that cause harm. In order to obtain a human life endowed with all the freedoms and advantages for

Dharma practice, we must also observe the precepts, accumulate merit, and have pure motivations and aspirations.

Take a look at what we do and say in our daily lives. Can we really observe our Buddhist vows? After careful examination, we may find our chance of obtaining another perfect human rebirth to be extremely remote. And even if we do observe the relevant vows that enable us to create the causes for necessary freedom, the question remains as to how many virtuous acts we have been performing to accumulate merit, and whether we have altruistic motivations in whatever we do. These two aspects greatly influence the character of our future lives. Only by perfecting our actions and thoughts related to the three aspects of vows, merit, and aspirations can we obtain a human life endowed with both freedoms and advantages. If we do not make full use of this life but waste it on worldly matters, our chance at liberation will slip away. And we may have to wait a long time to gain the freedoms and advantages we are enjoying now.

In the autumn of 1993, I went with three young monks to the Derge Printing House to buy Buddhist books for the Larung Buddhist Institute. When we passed my home village on the way, an old man donated a piece of land he had inherited as an offering for me to build a Dharma center (which is now the Tashi Triling Retreat Center). Having heard his wish, the other three monks also expressed their wishes to be my driver, my attendant, and the donor of roasted barley flour to the center after its establishment.

The young monk who wished to be my attendant was from the Qinghai province. I met him a year earlier when I was a guest teacher at a monastery in his home region. He had great confidence in His Holiness Jigme Phuntsok Rinpoche, and after I finished teaching at the monastery, went along with me to Larung. There he often zealously discussed with me his study plan. But he died unexpectedly less than three years later, at the age of only twenty-three. I met many young people like him, who were firm in their Buddhist beliefs and enthusiastic about spiritual practice. The Lord of Death, however, did not leave them with much time to do what they wanted. Thus, it is never too early for spiritual practice.

My best friend Tulku Rebu Dorje studied together with me at Larung. We once shared the same aspiration to go on a retreat at Mount Tsingphu, where Padmasambhava practiced. After graduation, however, I followed my root teacher His Holiness Jigme Phuntsok Rinpoche's advice to devote my life to teaching. Time has slipped away ever since, and I am afraid I might never have the chance to achieve my earlier ambition. Tulku Rebu Dorje, on the other hand, did not manage to go to Mount Tsingphu either. Instead, he has been in retreat in a secluded place among the hills behind Larung for almost two decades. For me, it is still both admirable and enviable.

Ephemeral and unpredictable, life is always changing and we do not always achieve what we want. Still we should never forget how fortunate we are to have this precious existence. Enlightening it with a more abiding purpose is what we all should endeavor to do in order to make full use of it.

What Makes You a Buddhist?

I often meet people who are attracted to the Buddhist ideas of compassion and bodhichitta, but who do not have the urge to take refuge in Buddhism due to a lack of insight into the teachings. As a result, I would like to talk about what taking refuge in Buddhism means for your life, and why it is necessary if you want to travel on the Buddhist path.

Today's world benefits enormously from technological advances and material riches. Nonetheless, people do not seem to be all that happy. It appears that material development has failed to eliminate people's inner suffering at its root. If we search the whole world for happiness, we will find Buddhism can truly help us attain inner peace and joy.

Growing up in the Tibetan region, I know very well how much Tibetans struggle with impoverishment. In terms of material scarcity, they are no different from people elsewhere. However, under the influence of Buddhism, they almost always remain content and peaceful with what they have. In summertime, on the wonderful grasslands of the high plateau, people gather to sing and dance, and they remain cheerful regardless of their harsh living conditions. Their carefree spirit is rarely seen in other places with a much higher living standard, where the incidence of suicide, for example, is not uncommon. Since almost everyone in the world fears death, choosing such a way to end one's life can only be reflective of how unbearable their inner suffering must be. It is for the sake of leading a truly happy life that I hope people can gain at least some understanding of Buddhism, even if they are not Buddhists.

As a Buddhist monk, I know Buddhism is by no means associated with superstition or nihilism as perceived by some people. Conversely, the teachings by our teacher, the Buddha Shakyamuni, emanated from his vast compassion and profound wisdom. They are greatly beneficial to all beings, especially at the moment of death. When death approaches, what wealth and power can do to help the dying process is limited to material things.

I have a young student who studies in Europe. A few years ago when visiting, she told me a story. One of her classmates came from a prestigious family and was incredibly wealthy. Not long ago, the father of the classmate was diagnosed with leukemia. Having heard the news, the family became very saddened, as did the father, who lived in great pain in the shadow of death. The wealth and status he possessed did not help relieve his suffering. Instead, his intense clinging to them made him even more miserable.

As a result of this incident, my student felt that wealth and status, the lifetime pursuit for most people, provided little consolation when one is dying. She said that she would return to China after finishing her study and live a simple life focused on learning and practicing Buddhism. She is from a well-off family and has lived a comfortable life. I was quite amazed that, at the age of only seventeen, she would have such mature insight into life.

How might a Buddhist face death? Here is another story of one of my students. She was a devoted practitioner and had been practicing Dharma for some years. Then she was diagnosed with advanced cancer. During the last days of her life, she did not panic. Instead, she calmly made the necessary arrangements in time, offering all her Buddha statues and pictures to her spiritual friends while keeping only her root teacher's image by her pillow. Fearful that painkillers might interfere with her thinking and impede her chances of obtaining a favorable rebirth, she requested not to be given any injections for pain relief. She also asked her family to keep her grandson away at her final moment, as she was very much attached to him. Although her family members were not Buddhists, they nonetheless agreed to do what she asked.

On her deathbed, her daughter called me. I asked her to place the phone by her mother's ear. Then, through the phone, I performed a transference ritual and recited some sacred names of buddhas and bodhisattvas for about thirty minutes. Then her family saw that she placed her palms together and passed away peacefully. Deeply impressed, her daughter, her son-in-law, and other family members started to develop faith in Buddhism. Later, when I visited the city where they lived, the whole family took refuge in the Three Jewels and became devoted Buddhists, just as the mother once did.

In the not-too-distant future, we all must meet death. The above two stories offer you a glimpse of how Buddhadharma and its incredible blessing power can help one navigate the dying process, as well as to live more meaningfully. In particular, Buddhadharma is the only support for one's liberation at the final and the most crucial moment. Therefore, for joyful living and ultimate spiritual liberation, may all of us devote some time to understanding Buddhism.

The first step on the Buddhist path is to take refuge in the Three Jewels. I often hear a saying that there is no need for the refuge ritual provided one has the Buddha in mind. Indeed, it is great to have the Buddha in mind, as this is the result of one's karmic connection with Buddhadharma and merit accumulated in the past. However, this in itself is not sufficient to make one a Buddhist. Any beginner who wants to traverse the Buddhist path must start with the formal refuge ritual. Imagine that you, for the first time in your life, bow and make offerings to sublime Buddha images, with keen devotion and in the presence of your teacher. Then you join your hands together and follow the teacher reciting the refuge verses, making vows to take refuge in the teacher, the Buddha, the Dharma, and the Sangha from now until complete enlightenment. That in itself will bring a tremendous transformation to your mind. And it is only through this refuge ritual that you become a genuine Buddhist. It is also essential to take the refuge vow.

According to the great Indian sage Atisha, the refuge vow is the basis of the laypeople's vow, bodhisattva vow, and tantric vow, all of which can only be received through specific rituals. In other words, without the refuge vow, it is impossible for one to receive all the other vows. Without those other vows, it is impossible for one to practice many methods of Dharma. And without practicing these, it is impossible for one's mind to be in tune with the teachings and eventually achieve liberation. In this respect, refuge is the gateway to all methods of Dharma.

Atisha had a famous saying: "Refuge is what makes Buddhism different from other faiths and beliefs." After his arrival in Tibet, his preaching at almost every Dharma gathering started with taking refuge. For this he was called "the Pandita of Refuge." Revered as a great Buddhist master in both India and Tibet, Atisha was instrumental in the eleventh-century revival of Buddhism in Tibet. The strong emphasis on refuge placed by such a master shows how crucial refuge is to Buddhist practice.

Among those who resist the idea of taking refuge are also people who do not understand the refuge vow and are concerned about the potential restrictions by the vow on their actions. The refuge vow stipulated by the Buddha is meant to serve as guidance for beginners. It is both straightforward and easy to observe for anyone who desires liberation. The essential part of the vow is to have unflinching faith in one's teacher and the Three Jewels and to refrain from abandoning the teacher and the Three Jewels under any circumstances, even if doing so will put one's life at risk. If one has such faith and resolution, one is ready to take refuge in Buddhism.

On the other hand, I do not believe that a person can be defined as a true Buddhist without genuine faith in the Three Jewels, even if one has undergone the refuge ritual, received a certificate and a Dharma name, and so on. In Tibet, people do not have refuge certificates, but most of them are faithful and devoted Buddhists. Therefore, when one takes refuge, faith in the Three Jewels must come first, avoiding overemphasis on formalities.

The Three Jewels in which one takes refuge refer to the Buddha, the Dharma, and the Sangha. Going for refuge in the Buddha, one seeks for and relies on no other guides but the Buddha and all other buddhas of the past, present, and future. Going for refuge in the Dharma, one seeks and practices no other ways but the eighty-four thousand methods of Dharma transmitted by the Buddha for the benefit of all beings, including the methods taught by Hinayana, Mahayana, and Vajrayana Buddhism. Going for refuge in the Sangha, one seeks no other spiritual companions on the path other than monastic members who follow the teachings of the Buddha. More specifically, the Sangha refers to a group of four or more monastic members in Hinayana Buddhism, while any enlightened person can be called the "Jewel of the Sangha" in Mahayana Buddhism.

Since one becomes a Buddhist after going through the formal refuge rite, they should start to learn Buddhadharma through hearing, contemplation, and practice in order to blend the teachings with their mental continuum. Importantly, one should first generate renunciation, a mind that has no desire for and attachment to any temporal pleasures and enjoyment in the six realms, but only yearns for liberation from samsara. Renunciation is like the philosopher's stone, turning all the virtue and merit we accumulate into the cause of liberation.

It is certainly best if we can stay away from all worldly concerns and practices with intense focus like Milarepa. However, this is hardly possible for most people, even including some monastics. So, if you cannot abandon all worldly concerns, you should at least bear in mind that liberation is the most important and ultimate goal of your life. If you practice step by step and persevere, your attachment to and desire for worldly things will subside gradually until you reach the final goal of liberation. Imagine that we want to travel to Lhasa. To fulfill the goal, we need to first set Lhasa as our destination. Then we take steps toward it and do not waver regardless of any obstacles we may encounter. With perseverance, we will be able to reach Lhasa one day. Similarly, if our focus is wealth and power and other worldly concerns, no matter what we practice, liberation will never be within reach.

Once we have generated renunciation, we should further generate bodhichitta, the foundation of Buddhahood. By bodhichitta we refer to the altruistic aspiration. One takes refuge in the Three Jewels and practices Dharma not only for one's own joy and liberation, but also for all beings' attainment of Buddhahood. For beginners, bodhichitta is not easy to arouse. Thus, Patrul Rinpoche, in his *Words of My Perfect Teacher*, teaches us how to cultivate bodhichitta gradually. One of the methods is to start with our loved ones and try to generate compassion and bodhichitta toward them. Next, we extend our compassion and bodhichitta to people to whom we feel no natural attachment and with whom we have no relationship. And finally, we grow compassion and bodhichitta toward those who have done harm to us. Through this gradual process, bodhichitta will eventually grow in us, and with bodhichitta as a mental support, every virtuous act we do becomes the seed of attaining Buddhahood.

Both renunciation and bodhichitta should be present in our motivation when we go for refuge. If one goes for refuge with only wealth, family, career, and so forth in mind, their motivation deviates from the right path of refuge and Dharma practice. In light of their significance, Tsongkhapa, in his famous work *The Three Principal Aspects of the Path*, elaborates on the three most pivotal elements leading to complete enlightenment: renunciation, bodhichitta, and uncontrived insight into emptiness.

Therefore, as a Buddhist, one should also abstain from killing, for it is contrary to the very idea of compassion and bodhichitta. Some people regard all human beings as equal but do not think there should be equality between animals and humans. This attitude reveals their lack of insight into various forms of life. If one examines carefully, they will find that animals do not differ in the way they feel joy and pain even though they are unable to speak to us in human language. When animals are cold, they gather to warm each other, while on hot days they search for cool places to stay. I have been promoting and performing animal release in different regions for some years. I often observe that those cattle and sheep in slaughter-houses show great terror when seeing others of their kind being killed ahead of them. Some of them cry out of fear just like humans, and some even kneel down before the people about to kill them. From the Buddhist perspective, if we only talk about equality among people but do not treat animals equally, it is not an expression of unbiased compassion.

Taking the life of any sentient being is not just in violation of compassion and bodhichitta. It can also cause ill effects under the law of cause and effect. Patrul Rinpoche said that killing one being requires five hundred lives of one's own to repay. And the *Sutra of a Hundred Actions* says: "Even after a hundred *kalpas* (eons), beings' actions are never lost. When the conditions come together, their fruit will fully ripen." Thus, killing without subsequent confession will give rise to painful effects that impact the killer. For the sake of ourselves and other beings, we should do our best to abstain from killing.

I also hope that people refrain from eating meat after taking refuge if possible. Not eating meat is a common practice adopted by different lineages of Buddhism. In most regions, it is relatively easy to rely on a pure, vegetarian diet. Modern science also proves the health benefits of a vegetarian diet. From the Buddhist perspective, a vegetarian diet is not only beneficial for health and longevity, but also conducive to favorable rebirth. If one cannot completely refrain from the consumption of meat at the beginning, they should eat only three kinds of "pure meat": (1) the unseen (meat that one has not witnessed killed specifically for their consumption), (2) the unheard (meat that one has not heard killed specifically for their consumption), and (3) the unsuspected (meat that one has not suspected was killed specifically for their consumption). While the karmic effect of eating these three kinds of "pure meat" is still grave, it is much less severe than if one participated in the killing.

Some people get used to eating meat every day, and it is hard for them to change their diet all at once. In this case, they should start with eating less meat every day. After that, they may try not to eat meat on Buddhist holy days. As a next step, they might consider a vegetarian-only diet during the Month of Miracles (the first Tibetan month) and the month of the Buddha turning the Dharma Wheel (the sixth Tibetan month). Through these progressive steps, they can ultimately quit eating meat. Eating less meat is also an effective way to save animal lives. I hope that all people of Buddhist faith can achieve this.

Finally, as a Buddhist one must practice diligently. Otherwise, one cannot benefit from the Dharma in the truest sense. Our behavior and mental states will remain the same year after year. And when we finally meet death, we will only have regret for not making any spiritual progress. Some people like to think that they do not have time right now and would rather wait till their retirement to practice. Life changes with every second that goes by. It is hard to say how much longer we will live. If we do not take the opportunity and practice right now, we may never get the chance to practice at a later time.

A while ago, Khenpo Darsen from the Tashi Triling Retreat Center was invited to recite Buddhist texts as a rebirth blessing for an old man who was dying. The man told Khenpo that he was very regretful. Instead of practicing Dharma, he committed many negative deeds in his younger years. Now that he already felt tremendous agony, he feared that he might fall to a lower rebirth where the suffering would be much more severe if he were to die soon. He prayed for Khenpo to help him live longer, even just for one more year. If so, he promised that he would do nothing but engage in Dharma practice to avoid a lower rebirth. Unfortunately, the man died soon after Khenpo Darsen's return to Tashi Triling.

Having heard the news, I felt extremely sad. One day, we all will die. Since we have the good fortune of being connected with the Buddha's teachings in this life, we should make the best use of our life by putting the teachings into practice, and practicing well.

PART 2

Escaping the Traps of Spirituality

What Do We Actually Renounce?

We often talk about integrating the Buddhist teachings into our lives. Surprisingly, however hard we try, spiritual practice often remains separated from our everyday routine. We feel good about ourselves when meditating, reciting sutras, and smiling at others, thinking that we have done well in putting Buddhadharma into practice to benefit ourselves and others. But when we are dejected, angry, in pain, or wronged, we tend to forget the teachings, and all except the intense sense of humiliation and frustration becomes blurry in our mind's eye. As a result, some might wonder whether the various methods our teachers have taught really work.

Why does spiritual practice fail to change our lives consistently? Why do those means and methods that have successfully transformed many people's destinies and enabled them to attain freedom and enlightenment never take effect on us? The answer probably lies in our excessive clinging to life. Consciously or subconsciously, every aspect of life—career, family, money, fame, and relationships—is of great significance to us. To make us feel secure, we want to keep all of them under control. Not only do we spend our time and energy on achieving this goal, but we also hope to boost our reassurance with spiritual practice. Regardless, life is like sand in our hands—the tighter we hold it, the quicker we lose it.

Spiritual practice loses its true purpose if it is only intended to fortify our egos and to give us extra assurance. The practice will become incoherent and distorted, unlikely to be rewarding in a life that is by nature impermanent. However, if we can loosen our clinging, take what comes to us more lightheartedly, and focus on practice itself, our lives will become better. True change will start to manifest itself, and we will get a first taste of freedom arising from detachment.

To learn to take it easy is therefore the first step of Buddhist practice. As we get used to tension and confrontation, we are always uptight about ourselves, others, and our environment. We do not like to live a life outside of our control, and the slightest sign of uncertainty is enough to make us restless. We keep ourselves busy and act like lifeguards, being in a state of constant vigilance and always anticipating disaster. Even if we take a physical rest, our mind remains unsettled between hope and fear. Many people even calculate to the point of being paranoid. When things go smoothly, we hope that the prospects remain rosy but we fear they will not. When things go wrong, we fear that they may get worse but we hope not. We cling to everything in life and intend to safeguard what we have. If under usual circumstances we are already neurotic, imagine how panicked we might be when encountering real misfortunes.

We live as if carrying a heavy stone on our head—whose weight can almost crush us—and the world dwindles to only problems. When we experience difficulties, we will perceive ourselves all the more as the world's most unlucky and wretched person. This mental state of self-pity amplifies our sense of justification to blame, to criticize, and to take revenge. As we do so, we forget life in itself is changeable and somewhat chaotic, filled with joy and sorrow. To make it more orderly or predictable is simply a vain attempt even if we dedicate our entire life to it. Therefore, Buddhist practice is meant to help us learn loosening-up, drop confrontation, accept uncertainty, and live with complete openness. Some call this mental state "the great ease of the mind."

When I was seventeen years old, I was on a retreat for the preliminary practices of the Great Perfection—called *Dzogchen* in Tibetan— under the guidance of Khenpo Tsewang Jigme. Both excited and nervous, I meditated in my small room day and night without sleep.

Initially, it went well. But soon obstacles arose when I started to meditate on the impermanence of life. Sitting in the same posture for quite some time, my body became tense and rigid. Contemplating impermanence also depressed me. Both my physical and mental states were not conducive to mental clarity, and signs of spiritual progress failed to emerge. I was both mortified and anxious.

One day, in a daze, I went out of my room aimlessly despite being in retreat, hoping to ease my anxiety. When Khenpo Tsewang Jigme heard about it, he called me over. "My boy," he said, "you should open the window and simply gaze into the vast, tranquil sky. Try to relax yourself as much as possible while doing so. Let your mind slowly dissolve into the sky and just rest there." I did accordingly and was soon out of the quandary, experiencing at last the absolute nature of the mind as clear and vast as the sky after rain.

Khenpo Tsewang Jigme's precious teaching has accompanied me ever since. Be relaxed and stay open, neither chasing thoughts nor anticipating any result but simply being aware. This is indeed the most important Buddhist practice.

More than twenty-five hundred years ago, when he looked up and saw the morning star, the Buddha Shakyamuni attained complete enlightenment under the bodhi tree where he meditated. After his awakening, the first words he uttered were that all sentient beings possess an innate mind of perfect bodhichitta. However greedy, ruthless, treacherous, or ignorant we have been, it is always with us and will never diminish. The practice is not for us to achieve or prove anything. Rather, it puts us at ease, enabling us to slowly and subtly get in touch with our innate mind.

It has been hard for us to see the innermost mind, as our usual way of living pulls us away from it. Many behaviors, especially the mental habits such as hope, fear, tension, aggression, complacence, irresponsibility, and self-righteousness, lead us to repeatedly fall into a trap. In order to get out of this mental trap, we have to change our behaviors through practice, slowly but surely.

Desire for comfort and aversion to misery are perhaps what is engrained most deeply in people's minds. This mental habit is not a problem in itself, just as our aspirations to be freed from suffering and to seek liberation are some of its manifestations. The real problem is that many of us are obsessed with it. Even slight discomfort will drive us to look for solace without giving ourselves room to experience. We turn on heating if cold, air conditioning if hot; we are addicted to driving, rarely walking around under the sun or in the rain. In the process of looking for material comfort, we miss the experience of the seasons and their joy. And we become weaker and more touchy.

Sometimes, this mental attitude is termed self-indulgence, which is usually associated with luxury and extravagance. But the truth is that everyone, albeit to a lesser extent for some, is inclined to experience this, as it is an expedient way to evade anxiety. When people feel lonely, depressed, or stressed, they might drink, overeat, go shopping, or talk for hours on the phone. They might also spend long hours surfing the web or vegetating in front of the TV, trying to avoid their real feelings. Doing so in turn results in a host of new problems. They intend to keep themselves away from emotional afflictions but in effect exchange one for another. This chain reaction further aggravates their fright.

In the old days, reading, writing, and other cultured hobbies were common ways to uplift the spirit and to cultivate the mind. These things are no longer popular, as people have become far less patient and get bored easily. Life is ephemeral like morning dew, but we act as if it does not move fast enough. Our obsession with material comfort is so deeply engrained in our minds that we want to simply avoid any feeling of dissatisfaction or inconvenience. We are constantly in search of consolation and expedience and always believe that we can find them.

Many people thus blame material prosperity for the increasing sense of dissatisfaction, inner hollowness, and other emotional problems they experience in modern life. But this is not necessarily true. To some extent, material things have influence over people. But ultimately, it is our own mind that plays the pivotal role. We are more afflicted because, with more material richness, there are more things in our lives to which we are attached. In the past, one might have found it hard to let go of a single watch. But now they may also have houses, cars, and savings in mind that worry them. Material affluence also offers people more options to escape from afflictions, allowing them to change more frequently their way of dealing with unhappiness. But by doing so, they become more easily dissatisfied and frustrated, and an inner hollowness follows.

When we were kids, a candy drop or a new dress could delight us immensely. When we received these gifts from our parents or others, we would feel thankful and say "thank you." We would cherish the sweet, and savor it slowly with our whole heart. We would appreciate the new dress and compliment it sincerely. But when we grow up, things that we regard as gifts become necessities, as we take more and more of them for granted. We think we deserve many things because we are smart, able, and hardworking. Nevertheless, there are many smart people in this world. There are also many who are able, let alone those who work hard. Just look at construction workers onsite—don't they work harder than we do? However, not all who are brighter, abler, and more hardworking live better than us. We are just luckier, but we forget to be grateful.

I am not saying that we should put our heads in the sand and endure suffering blindly. In fact, the issue is not whether we choose to suffer or not. The Buddha has already shed light on the fact that all impermanent things are suffering. Since nothing in this world can last, everything we own and experience in life inevitably alludes to uncertainty. There are also other kinds of suffering in life, ranging from gross to subtle, intense to moderate. We may call them loneliness, fear, resentment, or sadness and so on. They accompany our transient lives, regardless of our capability to manage the way we live. While we are supposed to be familiar with suffering, ironically, we never dare to take a close look at suffering itself.

I have had four major experiences related to illness, each of which deepened my awareness and insight into suffering. At age ten I was infected with chicken pox. Many children in the village died after contracting the disease. The locals believed that it was fatal for a chicken pox patient to drink water before skin lesions had crusted over, which usually took several days after lesions appeared. So, I was not allowed to drink during the period. Lying in bed and seeing others drinking, I hoped earnestly that I would get better soon. I thought I would be happy again if I could drink plenty of water.

When I was around eleven years old, my legs were severely burned during a tent fire. The village where I lived was remote and I could not get proper medication. The wound on my legs had undergone prolonged inflammation. Occasionally, a community veterinarian came and disinfected the wound. It really hurt when he did so. For almost a year I was bedridden. The villagers believed that I would have a limp after recovery, but that did not concern me at all. I only worried that I had missed lots of fun time. As soon as I was able to get out of bed, I went to play immediately despite a limp.

When I was eighteen years old, I was a guest student at the Dzogchen Shri Singha Institute and became quite frail due to malnutrition and exhaustion. Consequently, I suffered from acute stomach inflammation and was bedridden for about two weeks without any sign of recovery. The prospect of imminent death in a foreign place did not frighten me, as every aspiring Buddhist practitioner in Tibet is prepared to die anytime, anywhere. If I had to die so young, my only regret at the time was that there were still many precious Buddhist teachings that I had not yet learned.

In 1990, at age twenty-seven, a major heart attack brought me to the brink of death and caused me to spend months in intensive care. It has since left me with chronic heart disease and painful recurrences. The illness has nonetheless lent me a helpful hand in comprehending life's fragility and fleetingness, and it also has helped me to generate renunciation and compassion. Death can catch us at any moment, leaving us no choice but to depart. Being seriously ill has enabled me to understand the suffering of others: the miserable young man whose legs were amputated, the defenseless yak fearfully waiting for its turn to be killed in the slaughterhouse, the mother desperately searching for her child in the ruins after an earthquake, and so on. Through suffering I felt strongly connected with these people and animals. What I experienced was essentially the same as they did.

My four major encounters with illness somehow represent four kinds of attitude when people face suffering. Some hope suffering to end as soon as possible so that they will live happily thereafter. Some try to make the best out of life by having fun while at the same time enduring suffering. Some are not fearful of suffering, but suffering becomes a hindrance to their spiritual quest. And some embrace suffering and transform it into opportunities that lead to spiritual liberation.

A student once told me about an experience she had. Someone once took advantage of her and badly hurt her. If it had happened earlier, her life would have been turned completely upside down and she would have panicked, trying her best to take revenge or to make up for her loss. This time she was determined to act differently, not wanting to blame others or herself, but to relax and keep herself open to directly experience the pain with clear awareness. To her amazement, she felt something tender in her even though she felt afraid and dejected: the tenderness of her compassion for herself, for the person who hurt her, and for all other beings. In the end, what she had struggled hard to build was utterly unreliable and fragile, unable to withstand even a single blow. For the first time in her life, she had a taste of what renunciation really meant.

Usually when people experience suffering, their heart becomes smaller and their mind becomes narrower. They act as if hiding inside a walnut in the hope that the hard shell will protect them. And doing so only makes them more depressed and strained. It would be better for them to open up and to face pain, to let the intense feeling destroy deeply rooted ideas and mental propensities. Only then will the innate mind or its derivatives of compassion, renunciation, and relative bodhichitta have the chance to shine.

Egocentricity is another obstinate habit of ours. Although we know from the teachings of the Buddha that attachment to a self is the origin of suffering, we remain egoistic, self-conscious, and self-righteous, always blaming others for our problems. Grasping in itself implies our inner fear. An infant always clenches his fists on his arrival in this unknown world. We do so too when feeling uneasy or frightened. As our whole life is overshadowed by the fear of loss, we keep snatching, gripping, and hoarding, never feeling content.

The Buddha teaches us to practice generosity and, through giving, to alleviate our sense of deprivation. If someone needs food and we have food, we should give it to them; if someone needs clothes, medicine, money, consolation, and care and we are able to give, we should help. There was once a child who went to the Buddha for a present. The Buddha said to him, "If you say 'I do not want it,' I will give you a present." The child, afraid of getting nothing if he said so, did not obey. But the Buddha insisted. After several rounds of going back and forth, the child finally conceded to the Buddha, albeit reluctantly, and he got what he wanted. Later the Buddha said to his disciples, "This boy has been miserly over many lives. He had never even said 'I do not want it,' let alone let go of anything. By having said so today he has planted a seed of giving and relinquishing for potential liberation."

Hold or relinquish—it seems like a serious choice. Yet in reality, it is not up to us to pick and choose. Willingly or not, our entire life is dominated by loss. Youth, joy, tears, success, failure, love, hatred, and even the entire world, will eventually leave us. The key of giving is not about how much help we can offer to others, but about learning to let go of our own clinging. Over time, our bodily actions can influence our frame of mind. Generally speaking, to let go is relatively easy for those who are generous. A thief once asked a master how to attain liberation. The master asked whether he had any special skill. The thief thought for a while and said that he could do nothing but steal. "Great!" The master replied, "Just steal a 'self' from yourself and you will attain liberation."

Take a look at yourself. If you look carefully, you will see you have already lost so much, and many things once deemed indispensible to your life are no longer there. But you are still alive, still able to experience life's joy and wonder. Suddenly, you will find that you have nothing to lose right from the start.

We regard ourselves as experienced and knowledgeable about everything. But most of the time, we see the world through conceptualization and association. White is perceived as purity; roses are romance; beach is holiday; raining is having no taxi. Thoughts induced by association play a more important role than the specific object that induces such association. To see and to know the world through a broader perspective requires both courage and forbearance. However, we are obstinate and lazy, either induced by self-righteousness or the other way around. And we believe this shows our passion and affirmation for life.

Whenever we see something, our first reaction is to judge: right or wrong, beneficial or harmful, agree or disagree. Then we start to make comments like a chatty commentator. This tendency to rush to a judgment, together with our biased perspective, prevents us from seeing things clearly.

One of my students told me about an experiment in which he participated during an executive training course, meant to highlight the power of selective attention. They were shown a video of a team of people wearing black and a team wearing white and were asked to count the number of times the white team passed a basketball among them.

Having watched the video attentively, all the students were able to count the white team's passes. Then the lecturer smiled, asking whether any of them noticed a gorilla.

What? *A gorilla?*

No one in the class had spotted it—and they were sure there wasn't one. The lecturer then played the video again. This time, they no longer directed their attention to the people in white passing the ball, but instead really watched the entire video. Indeed, a person wearing a gorilla suit and mask walked in and even did some karate moves in the middle of the group for a while before leaving. Everybody saw it this time.

Isn't this an interesting experiment? We think of ourselves as sharp, observant, and discerning, but we only see what we want to see and hear what we want to hear instead of what we *can* see and hear.

The Buddha teaches us to see and to listen with an open mind. Only in this way can we truly see and hear. At the first turning of the Wheel of the Dharma at Sarnath's Deer Park in Northern India, the Buddha's first teaching was on suffering—this is suffering; suffering must be recognized. When we are in pain, we should know that it is nothing but suffering, not confusing it with something else. Some biases and misunderstandings can be easily corrected, provided we make some mental adjustments. But some false assumptions, formed many generations ago and passed down to our time, have become common sense and prevailing wisdom. If we want to live more truthfully, sometimes we have to act as if we are without common sense or even go against it. Take a look at those practitioners who completely renounce their worldly lives. They reject wrong views and refuse to follow the crowd. They feel they have been fooled long enough, and in order to get out of this deceptive game, they want to learn and experience things earnestly with an open heart and mind. Although not all of us can be so determined, we can at least acknowledge our ignorance and no longer try to be obstinate, lazy, and complacent about a "second-hand" life. To rest our mind for a quiet moment each day is for us to truly see, listen, and feel.

Self-righteousness not only sets us apart from the present, but it also makes us vulnerable to getting hurt and easily hurting others. We are self-absorbed and often care too much about our ways of doing things. On TV, there is always someone talking about how they cook, apply makeup, lose weight, achieve success, and manage money. In public areas, people wear the same hairstyle; all seem only to be interested in talking on mobile phones; and their mood goes up and down in tandem with the stock market. Still they think that they are unique and that their ideas and way of life are the best. This self-cherishing prevents us from getting along and communicating properly with others. Many of us even think that what we do and say not only is right but also has to be right. If others do not concur, we feel hurt. When facing people, things, or situations, we like to draw a quick conclusion between right or wrong. Otherwise, we feel useless and insecure. Consequently, our beliefs, ideals, and values are often used to reinforce our egos and to ostracize others. Just look at quarrels, conflicts, and wars—all the parties involved believe that they are right while the opponents are wrong.

Sometimes, self-righteousness manifests itself as low self-esteem, when we insist there is nothing good about ourselves. Like vanity, low self-esteem turns us blind, preventing us from seeing ourselves clearly and from communicating with the outer world. Without mutual communication and connections, we feel lonely and isolated. Our sense of "being the only one" further dramatizes how we feel. For instance, you will be pleased if you are among half of the participants who have passed the exam. But if you know that you are the only one who has passed, you might feel not just pleased but almost delirious. On the other hand, if you fail the exam while half of the participants too have failed, you will feel dejected. But if you are the only one who has failed, you might think that you are the most unfortunate person. When depressed, lonely, and isolated, we are inclined to perceive ourselves as the most miserable, although our situation is actually much better than we think.

Many people commit suicide because they cannot bear their suffering anymore. Whenever I hear such news, I am extremely sad. Death is a big unknown and this unknown causes horror. The pains associated with the dissolving of the four elements at death are beyond imagination. Nevertheless, these people still choose to die. They must have suffered more than they could bear before suicide.

Suffering is universal, and it is not just the experience of a handful of people. There is no such thing as fate that tries to be your enemy, beat you down, and abandon you. Your experience is what all sentient beings have to go through. Therefore, you are not abandoned, and you should take it easy and learn to understand suffering through your own experience. You can learn to let go of your worries, self-pity, and judgment and get out of the self-invented circle of "right or wrong" and "able or unable" about yourself. You can step outside and appreciate the beauty of flowers and the freshness of the morning breeze. Although your pain might still be there and intense, it will no longer suffocate you and drive you to despair, for your heart has been opened.

For some of you, the sense of grievance, powerlessness, regret, shame, fear, or frustration is too real and intense to let go, even if you want to learn detachment. If so, you do not have to drop anything in a hurry. You are already so unhappy. There is no need to make your life more difficult. What a big heart you need to have in order to bear so much worry and sorrow. So why not give yourself a minute to close your eyes and imagine: Your heart is getting even bigger; it is resilient; slowly it holds you with tenderness; then it expands to embrace the whole room, the yard, streets, passersby, bridges, cities, rivers, mountains, the sky, the sun and the moon and the stars. Concentrate on that feeling of openness that seems to stretch infinitely. When you open your eyes again, you might feel better.

Ostensibly, we refuse to communicate because we think others do not understand us. In reality, we are projecting our own thoughts onto others. Our liking and disliking of others are simply a reflection of our mental attitudes toward ourselves. You do not want to understand others at all, so you think others will not understand you. You are fearful of becoming poor, so you hate to see the poor. You do not want to face shallowness, narrowness, and coldness in you, so you disdain others' shallowness, narrowness, and coldness. Therefore, we will not accept ourselves until we start to accept others. In order to train this mental openness, some practitioners intentionally keep company with difficult people. When India's Atisha came to Tibet, he took with him an ill-tempered and cantankerous man as his attendant, afraid that Tibetans were too kind and gentle to be the object of his mind training.

We all cherish ourselves and want to do good for ourselves. Paradoxically, our habitual tendencies make us look like fools. What we have been doing makes us more baffled and unhappier. To change these habits is what we call renunciation. Next time you are stuck in a traffic jam, watch how you react. Are you worried and restless? Do you look at your watch repeatedly and nervously? Do you call your friends to complain? Do you blame the policeman, the car, and the driver in front of you, or the traffic lights that are not working? Do you turn on the radio only to find that it annoys you even more? Just try to observe your reactions without judging or intentionally correcting them. To observe your own reactions instead of being overwhelmed by emotions is already a change. Again, another time when you are in a traffic jam, watch your reactions. Again and again, you repeatedly observe your reactions whenever you are in a traffic jam until one day you see your own absurdity, always reacting in the same fashion without any originality: complaining, looking at your watch, and calling friends. So, the next time you are in a similar situation, you may want to do something different: listen attentively to what is being broadcast on the radio, enjoy a song, have empathy with the anxious driver next to you, or rearrange your schedule due to the traffic jam. Doing this will help you learn to avoid making your life more difficult.

Cyclic existence is like inertia. Changing our habits with perseverance will weaken the great force behind it and slow down its momentum. Traditionally, renunciation refers to a mind that wearies of samsara and suffering and longs for happiness and liberation. As suffering originates from attachment, what we are meant to renounce is precisely attachment. Attachment can be anything and everything. This makes renunciation a task that demands focus and diligence in order to avoid traps.

Once a practitioner visited his master Jamyang Khyentse Wangpo, a renowned teacher, scholar, and *tertön* (treasure revealer) in nineteenth-century Tibet. On his way, he gave away everything he had, save his beloved wooden bowl. Upon arrival at the palatial residence of his master, he wondered, "People call my lama 'the one without possessions.' How come he lives in such a luxurious place?" Seeing this, Jamyang Khyentse Wangpo laughed, "You silly, judgmental fellow! My attachment to the gold, silver, and gems of the entire house is nowhere near your clinging to that wooden bowl." As soon as he said so, he snatched the practitioner's bowl and broke it on the floor.

Such is renunciation. It concerns one's inner mind rather than appearance.

The Ultimate Refuge of Life

I was born and grew up in a land nurtured by Buddhism. Like me, most people there are devoted Buddhists. The material comfort and pleasure of this and future lives are not what we seek. Life is rugged and Buddhist faith does not help improve our material well-being; nor does it make us feel spiritually superior or better protected, as all sentient beings are equally endowed with Buddha nature. What is in Buddhism that makes us content and peaceful even though we are impoverished and lead a wandering life?

It is the Buddha's teachings on impermanence and causality that give us great courage and hope. Even the most destitute and illiterate Tibetans have a deep conviction in the karmic law of cause and effect and are able to face changes in life without fear. Essentially the various emotional afflictions and struggles in our times are about fear of impermanence, and to escape this, people busy themselves with endless activities. Interestingly, some people live an unsettled life despite living in large mansions, while others live at ease despite being homeless.

Our aversion to impermanence is largely due to our misapprehension of life and the world around us. First, people perceive impermanence as being a kind of experience that can be eluded strategically. Anxious to ensure a steady life, we attempt to avoid change, unaware that by doing so we evade life itself. Life is change. If we pay a little more attention, it is not hard for us to see the pervasiveness of change: the shifts of the physical universe, seasons, people, our bodies, emotions, and thoughts are all part of this immense flux. Impermanence is not a short-lived transition; rather, it is the bare face of our entire life. Willingly or unwillingly, we have to keep it as our lifetime companion.

Secondly, people perceive impermanence as the cause of frustration and agony. If things remained constant, suffering could be avoided. But in reality, impermanence is neither good nor bad. It acts like a pendulum that can swing in either direction between gain and loss, but only for so long. Being happy or miserable is very much contingent on our perspective and mental attitude, not so much on impermanence itself. To a large extent, impermanence only shatters our delusion about security and certainty. A resolute belief may change. A loved one may leave. A healthy body may get sick. And a prosperous business may go bankrupt. When we face an imminent fall, we instinctively want to grasp at something. This is how grasping emerges. However, since what we want to grasp is intrinsically impermanent and consequently unreliable, our suffering ensues. It is our own grasping rather than impermanence that produces our suffering. To evade impermanence is thus both futile and unnecessary.

Acknowledging and accepting impermanence may not be easy at the beginning because for a long time we have been working hard to avert it. Impermanence is like the phantom of the opera, ugly by appearance but gentle within. Its face will always terrify us if we remain distant from it. But once we get close to it and understand it, we can easily befriend it.

People tend to ignore impermanence when life goes well, although improvement is also a display of impermanence. It is not until things turn sour that we suddenly notice it. In this seemingly harsh way, life is trying to remind us of our blindness to the illusory nature of security, and to the ever-changing nature of all phenomena. If we continue neglecting spiritual practice, our brief existence will be squandered on meaningless pursuits and anxieties.

My own first encounter with death was at around the age of seven. One day my grandmother suddenly fell ill, and the family was sobbing at her bedside. I loved my grandmother dearly and wanted to do something for her. So, I sneaked out every evening to a ruined *mani* mound outside the village—a mound of stones with the markings of the six-syllable mantra OM MANI PADME HUM, the heart mantra of the Bodhisattva of Compassion, Avalokiteshvara. I prostrated around the mani mound while at the same time chanting the six-syllable mantra. Dedicating the merit of what I did to my grandmother, I hoped that she would survive. Yet she died.

Following local custom, my family placed my grandmother's corpse on the back of a yak and took it to a nearby sky-burial ground where a sky-burial ceremony was performed for her. I did not join the final farewell. Instead, I went to the same mani mound and chanted the mantra again. From there I could see the sky-burial ground on the other side of the river. In the distance, vultures gathered aloft, more and more, circling in the hard, steely sky. A deep sense of sorrow came over me. Instead of crying, I continued chanting and prostrating, wishing that this modest merit might benefit my grandmother's rebirth. My grandmother's death instilled in me a profound sense of life's impermanence and sadness. It also made me appreciate the value of Buddhism and spiritual practice.

Impermanence is every practitioner's intimate friend, for it constantly reminds him to stay alert while furnishing encouragement and hope. Impermanence also reveals the possibility that everything can change. However serious the mistake we may have made in the past and however ignorant we are now, we can purify our past negative karma and gradually dispel our delusion.

Some people approach impermanence the other way around. Since all is impermanent and will disappear eventually, they think that we can do whatever we want without concern for consequences. They also think that it is senseless for us to pursue anything, as we can take nothing with us in the end. In order for us not to get lost in impermanence, the Buddha compassionately expounded another truth behind all phenomena—the karmic law of cause and effect.

To have confidence in cause and effect is not tantamount to believing in fate. Otherwise, we would not practice diligently and repent our negative actions, nor would we now seek complete enlightenment. Since all things are subject to constant change, there is no such thing as predestined fate. Each and every action will result in consequences, influencing our lives and others' as well. Wild grass sprouts and grows quickly while it takes a year for barley to flower and crop. Likewise, some effects of our actions will become immediate while others will take much longer to ripen. Ubiquitous, profound, and intricate, the law of cause and effect governs every phenomenon. The Buddha says that the entire causal chain behind a single phenomenon can only be discerned by beings who have attained complete enlightenment. What we normally see is just a small part of it.

If we understand that whatever we do will affect others and ourselves, we will naturally become responsible and no longer think and act myopically and recklessly. We will also develop further insights into the interdependence between people, as well as between people and the world. And the need to cultivate compassion becomes evident, too. If we hope to ultimately eliminate suffering, we should not harm others; if we want to be happy, we should create conditions to make others happy.

How the karmic law of cause and effect works is often interpreted as justice. Personally, I am not fond of the word "justice." It evokes punishment and sounds cold and distant. We do not believe that someone or something is out there praising or protecting us if we do the right things and punishing us if we do the wrong things. Instead, we are always our own master. The difficulties and pains we experience are simply the effects of our past deeds. If our attitude is positive, what we suffer will not only cancel out a past cause and effect, but will also create a virtuous cause leading to positive results. Therefore, suffering is not necessarily bad, since every experience in life can be an opportunity for enlightenment. The key lies in our own mental attitude when facing it.

The reason that we place great emphasis on mental attitude is that the true consequence of an action is largely determined by the motivation behind it. In Tibet, where the pursuit of spiritual liberation is the center of life, even a slight action is motivated by a wish to benefit all beings. Because of this vast attitude, even if one just places a small mani stone on top of a mani mound, one sows a seed of future liberation. If our attitude is vast enough to take into account the happiness of all sentient beings regardless of what we do, we will be able to withstand hardships and difficulties patiently.

In light of the law of cause and effect, if the effect of a past action is yet to ripen and you have not taken any measures to counteract it, it will surely ripen in your next life or in those to follow. Death only marks the end of this life. The unexhausted causes and effects will be carried forward to the next life, which, while bearing the old fruits, will simultaneously create new causes and effects. These are like waves, one after another without end, pushing life's endless cycle where the past, present, and future are connected by an unbroken causal chain rather than a "soul." Despite the stark independence of the present life from future lives in terms of their physical and mental manifestations, the present life forms the basis of future ones. Since karmic effects vary in their attributes and potencies, the resultant rebirths vary accordingly. This is how samsara's six realms came into being. The particular realm in which one takes rebirth depends entirely on the karmic effects one is bound to experience. As Guru Padmasambhava says, "If you want to know your past life, look at what you are now; if you want to know your future life, look at what you do now."

Today the subject of death has become taboo and many people avoid talking about it—and discussion about cyclic existence gets avoided as well. Whenever I mention cyclic existence, someone will challenge me by saying, "How am I going to believe in reincarnation if I have never witnessed it?" Or, "If I've already experienced reincarnation, why don't I remember it?" In fact, we do not always have to believe by seeing. For instance, we never doubt that we have ancestors several generations ago despite the fact that we have never met them. We have been told by scientists about millions of galaxies in the universe similar to the Milky Way to which our solar system belongs. Some are so far away that even the most advanced astronomical telescopes fail to spot them. Still we believe in their existence.

It is not necessary to be perplexed by our lack of memory about past lives. We can easily forget things that happened years, months, or days ago, or even what we have just done or said. So, it should not be surprising that you cannot remember your past lives. When you say "I don't believe in cyclic existence," perhaps you actually mean "I don't want to believe in cyclic existence." Perhaps the idea of it seems too far-fetched for you to grasp or you do not have the courage and curiosity to consider it a possibility. You also probably regard cyclic existence and death as being too distant from your daily life to spend much time thinking about them. Preoccupied with living, you have no time to think about the afterlife. But look at those around you—many of them died unexpectedly. You cannot be sure that you will be luckier. We Tibetans have a saying: "Tomorrow or the next life, we never know which might come earlier."

Some people equate the idea of reincarnation with superstition, rejecting it as irrational. Yet if we deny the reality of the law of cause and effect, we become lost in the face of impermanence. Family, career, and friendship will all leave us in the end. Ambition, ideology, and belief cannot stand up to time's scrutiny either. I am not suggesting that these things are of no value, but our sense of being goes far beyond them.

Modern life is filled with theoretical hypotheses, and I often wonder why people resist the idea of reincarnation. In a sense, it is no more preposterous than assuming the reality of tomorrow or next year. We are often very concerned with planning for our future, so why, then, do we not grant ourselves the chance to prepare for death and beyond? If there is indeed a next life, is it not something important for us to plan for?

Admittedly, our value system is an individual choice, and it is unwise to blindly follow others. However, being narrow-minded and dogmatic does not serve us well either. For those cynical about cyclic existence, I think a more pragmatic approach is to acknowledge their lack of understanding in this subject and take the chance to learn about it.

Many Tibetans place great emphasis on spiritual development. This is thanks to our deep conviction in impermanence and the karmic law of cause and effect. It is natural for us to take refuge in the Buddha, Dharma, and Sangha. Had Shakyamuni not attained complete enlightenment through his own efforts, and had he not compassionately shared with us this uncontrived wisdom, we would probably have remained blind in our quest, not knowing where we came from, who we are, and where we are going. For people who have not benefited from his teachings, some may think that they cannot do much about life even if they lead a meaningless one. I would have been one of those people if not for my exposure to the Buddha's teachings transmitted by his followers over generations. Because of this, my heart is filled with gratitude for the Three Jewels.

After the Buddha attained enlightenment, he discovered that all sentient beings possess a perfectly luminous, innate mind that can be awakened. This is indeed inspiring, for we would otherwise be ignorant of this innate goodness in us given our presently deluded state. The Buddha not only points out that all beings can achieve enlightenment, but also patiently teaches us how to remove delusion. He inspires us and encourages us, shares his teachings, and tells us how to verify them through practice and realization. He reveals the truth of life through different means tailored to individual mental qualities and habits. The longer we drift in the ocean of samsara, the worse our delusion becomes. Even the Buddha himself said that, among his countless past lives, he had been a white dog over many lifetimes. If the bones of all these dogs were piled up, it would be higher than Mount Sumeru, the central mountain in Buddhist cosmology. We are far more mired in the depths of samsara than the Buddha was before his enlightenment. If we desire change, we must rely on effective means. The process leading to enlightenment is like a map that guides us through a maze. Without the guidance of the Dharma, we become perpetually trapped.

Some followers of the Buddha are also said to be the embodiments of the Buddha. They come to us, train us, and fight with us. They ensure that we never lose perspective, even at our darkest and most uncertain moments. It is through them that we see the possibility of our own enlightenment.

The individual kingdoms of India during the time of the Buddha had many spiritual practitioners. It is said that while some of these practitioners had accomplished high levels of meditative concentration, only the Buddha had attained perfect and complete enlightenment and had seen the true face of all phenomena. Many, then, after seeking advice from the Buddha, came to see the defects in their previous practices. In order to achieve what the Buddha had accomplished, they decided to abandon their old ways and follow him. With reverence they expressed this unequivocal resolution in the Buddha's presence. Subsequently, thousands of practitioners expressed the same resolution in front of either the Buddha or his followers. The transmission of resolution from one person to another has since produced the Buddhist lineage.

When you have decided to open your mind and travel on the Buddhist path without bias, you must solemnly express your resolution through both body and speech in the presence of a member of the Sangha. It is not just a symbolic ceremony but has profound significance. Since Buddhist practices encompass the three aspects of one's body, speech, and mind, taking refuge with all these three aspects present sows an ideal seed of realization. Meanwhile, by taking refuge with a qualified teacher, your resolution will become part of the resolution of millions of practitioners of the past, present, and future. In this continuum of resolution that goes back to the Buddha, your resolution no longer stands alone. Just imagine how powerful this mental leverage can be.

After you have taken refuge in the Three Jewels, you will also receive the refuge vow. Among the three aspects mentioned, the mind is the primary driver. Actual refuge will only occur if you have genuine devotion to the Jewel of the Buddha as the actual refuge that shows you the path and teaches you; a deep conviction in the Jewel of the Dharma as the actual refuge that guides you to realize your own Buddha nature; and high respect for the Jewel of the Sangha as the actual refuge that accompanies you and protects you on the spiritual path.

In my childhood, Buddhist images, statues, scriptures, and monastic members were hardly seen. Yet people's faith in the Three Jewels never wavered. Many children including myself also knew at an early age how to pray to the Three Jewels, but many years later I found out that not everyone knew how to pray, and that many of them did not have the courage to admit their need for help. I myself liked to chant mantras, but the prayer beads were impossible to get at the time. In order to make them, I often climbed up the nearby hillsides together with other kids in the village to collect seeds from cypress trees. Then we made beads out of them. The seeds were extremely hard, and it was difficult to pierce them with a needle. Still, I always enjoyed doing it. Sitting cozily in the bush, I often started my day mending my ragged clothes, after which I made prayer beads. Slowly, the day went by in such simple delight.

I also learned how to chant sutras and prayers from the village elderly. The way they taught me could indeed be called "oral transmission." They were illiterate. So was I at the time. They recited the texts, which they themselves heard from others, sentence by sentence to me. I recited after them and memorized all the texts. However, some like the *Sutra of Tara* and the *Wishing Prayer of Dewachen* turned out to be chanted inaccurately by the elderly. It nonetheless made such an imprint on my mind that I sometimes still make mistakes while chanting those texts.

Throughout my life, Buddhism has brought me immense peace and joy. Nonetheless, taking refuge does not guarantee a life free of worry and hassle, nor does it mean that somebody will come to solve our problems when needed. I actually think that being a Buddhist entails tremendous courage. Buddhism does not promise us security and certainty. Actually, it shatters our illusion of security. Taking refuge means that we are finally determined to face up to any circumstances in life. Instead of seeking comfort or consolation and looking for other ways out, we are to live in the present. In Tibetan, Buddhists are called "inner seekers"—those who turn their minds inward in search of absolute truth.

The cultures of our modern era are generally characterized by pompousness, flamboyance, and unsettledness. Words like *reflection* and *introspection* can sound both alien and dull. However, Buddhist practice is essentially mindfulness, which amounts to a heightened awareness of ourselves and our environment.

We all tend to be enthusiastic about something new, and Buddhist practice is no exception. After having received brief advice, we may be full of expectations. We start a routine revolving around meditation, mantra recitation, and orderly eating and sleeping. By doing so we believe that life is finally put on the right track and that we are making progress. Sometimes we even feel that enlightenment itself appears to be within reach. But soon disappointment sets in. Life does not become more predictable. Neither do we realize the progress we aspired to quickly enough. Mind training forces us to constantly confront our true selves, and we find ourselves repeatedly and powerlessly returning to old patterns of behavior. Is this so-called Buddhist practice?

Indeed, Buddhist practice is not a dazzling magic show that excites and amazes us all along, nor is it a shield against daily hassles. It may even be more tedious than the daily trivia we try to evade. The practice is not supposed to enhance our lives or adorn our egos. If this were the case, the Buddha, when he was Prince Siddhartha Gautama, would not have abdicated his throne to become a self ordained monk. He was raised in the royal palaces built by his father, where he was shielded against all sufferings. One day he slipped out of the palace and saw the sick, the old, and the dead—the real faces of human life. Realizing that suffering eventually would not spare him either, he decided to abandon his life at the palace. Thus, our practice is about unchaining ourselves from self-deception.

Once we start the practice, we become aware how little we know about what we do, how we feel, and what we think. Habits conditioned over many lifetimes discourage us from simply being with ourselves. To be vigilant and mindful is thus rather challenging. It entails that we remain open to all situations without impulsive judgment, desire, and aversion. This makes us seemingly powerless. Yet mindfulness does not stop there. We must consciously observe how we try to look for alternatives but to no avail. Frankly speaking, this is not very pleasant for beginners. Previously, we could always resort to anxiety, harsh words, anger, self-criticism, and so on. We could always shout and yell, be overwhelmed by negative emotions, and refuse to see reality calmly. But with mindfulness, we realize that such actions and emotions can no longer be our resort.

It is a long-established tradition that spiritual practitioners must cultivate forbearance. In the context of Buddhist practice, it refers to mental openness and resilience that prevent one from reacting on impulse and being led by negative emotions. Not looking for immediate remedies, evasion, or solace, a practitioner tries to take a pause, to observe, and to directly experience each moment, and thereby see the truth of the matter.

Persistent mind training enables us to gradually acquire such openness. The hope and fear that often devour us are two sides of a coin. Fear comes with hope, evoking the desire to evade what is undesirable, which in turn fuels fear. Therefore, neither expecting nor resisting allows our mind to rest at ease. Only then can we possibly catch a glimpse of what really is behind the illusory façade of actions and thoughts that make us laugh or cry.

In order to avoid loneliness, people like to keep themselves busy. To turn our minds to Buddhadharma we need to be our own companions. On the path to enlightenment, we will surely fall prey to old propensities again and again. Nevertheless, we must keep practicing, never give up, and be courageous. We should always be grateful for the Three Jewels. Without their encouragement and inspiration, our strength and perseverance would wane. Taking refuge therefore is not just the beginning of the path; it is the entire path of spiritual liberation.

Bodhichitta, the Vast Attitude

Buddhists are people who have resolved to be with themselves on a more intimate level. This means two things: to be mindful of one's own actions and thoughts, and to be gentle to oneself. Vigilant mindfulness allows us to see our own narrowness, apathy, and confusion. We may think we are good enough, but through mindfulness, we find it is not at all true. And this is probably what makes so many Buddhists procrastinate when it comes to practice. Unlike talking high theories or performing rituals and charitable deeds pretentiously, facing one's own shortcomings does not please vanity or boost morale. However, some people go to the opposite extreme and the result of their vigilant mindfulness troubles them. Probing hard what is beneath their narrowness, apathy, and confusion, they become cynical and unfriendly due to their own self-criticisms.

Without mindfulness and introspection, we cannot ultimately dispel delusion; without gentleness and graciousness, there is only pain left in our practice. Love, compassion, sympathetic joy, and impartiality all arise from a gentle warm heart. To be loving and compassionate is a popular teaching, but this love and compassion should be directed to both others and oneself, and firstly to oneself. Without being loving and compassionate to oneself, it will be hard for one to do so for others. We should honor each momentary experience, value the insights gained through them, and acknowledge our weakness without losing self-esteem. Even if we see our faults, we remain content and appreciative. Doing so is essential to our practice because only by not giving up on ourselves will we not abandon others; only when we esteem our own feelings will we willingly develop empathy for others; only when we believe that we have the potential of attaining enlightenment will we believe that others, too, have such potential and eventually enter the Mahayana path.

Mahayana Buddhists aspire to practice Buddhadharma and attain Buddhahood for the ultimate liberation of all sentient beings. This vast attitude is called *bodhichitta* in Sanskrit. We have long wandered in samsara and have been well coached by greed, ignorance, and anger. Consequently, the generation of bodhichitta is easier said than done. Nonetheless, we should aspire to do so, even if our aspiration is not quite sincere or even in doubt. Our mind is extremely malleable, and provided we keep training it, things that are false can eventually become true. In time, a contrived aspiration can be transformed to veritable bodhichitta.

In Buddhist practice, bodhichitta is not empty rhetoric. It is based on the four boundless qualities of love, compassion, sympathetic joy, and impartiality, and involves detailed steps to arouse.

The Buddhist concept of love is driven by the wish that all beings be happy and enjoy the cause of happiness. This unconditional love can be cultivated through fostering one's ability to love, treating all beings with sincerity and good intent, and living in harmony with the environment. At the beginning, we are unlikely to extend love and kindness to all beings equally. So, our practice starts with wishing ourselves to be happy. With a sense of joy, we gradually extend our love and kindness to those close to us, then to strangers, then to people whom we dislike, and finally to all sentient beings.

Someone once told me that it is not difficult for him to mentally dedicate the merit of his good deeds to "all sentient beings," but when it comes to specific individuals such as their enemies, it becomes hard. Such a mental attitude is not unusual, as in their mind the term *sentient beings* is only a collective noun with no concrete meaning; or at least it does not encompass those they dislike. Therefore, it is important for us to expand our aspirations progressively. It is acceptable that we are biased and somewhat narrow, but we should not be negligent and self-deceiving.

Being kind to ourselves is not tantamount to self-indulgence. The latter squanders self-esteem rather than generating inner peace and joy. Being kind entails learning about ourselves through a gentle approach, observing with a sense of humor our hubris, ignorance, coldness, and stubbornness. Although our deficiencies can be obstinate, they are no more than ludicrous games played by our minds. Once we sort out the rules of the games, we will be able to resist their enticement and deception. Through mindfulness and vigilance, we will eventually know what brings about happiness and what causes suffering. In order to be happy, we will be cautious about what we do and think.

If we are sufficiently attentive and honest in observing ourselves, we will see how often we unintentionally harm others as well as ourselves. We like to exaggerate our feelings, especially negative ones, even though doing so aggravates our pain. Reluctant to open our heart, we are unwilling to forgive and refuse to face up. Instead, we choose to believe that we are deeply hurt, as it is sometimes much easier to dwell on miserable thoughts and emotions than to simply forgive. Without mindfulness, we are blind to the nature of reality and our true feelings. Our sadness, agony, and confusion are all for nothing.

Even if we mean no ill, we can still hurt others by what we do and say. But we tend to dismiss this kind of harm, claiming that we had good intentions regardless of the harm we have done in actuality. Actually, this is just another way of saying we are not ready to open up and communicate with others. The biggest dilemma for many is precisely this habitual mental closure, the unwillingness to communicate with others. Anything can be taken as a mental barrier between others and oneself and used as an excuse to reject communication. We may think we are on the right side of justice and moral decency, so we are justified in ignoring the harm that we have done. Or, we may think we have a better and more profound understanding of life and the universe, so we are reluctant to be friendly and pay due respect to people who do not share our beliefs.

The loving-kindness of Mahayana bodhisattvas is unconditional. We all have the potential to develop it, provided we are willing to allow into our hearts all those whom we wish to be happy. For us, *sentient beings* is not just a term. It represents numerous specific lives with whom we can build close emotional affinity.

If we find it hard to love ourselves, we can start with someone who is most able to evoke our tenderness and gratitude. After that, we can project this love and gratitude onto people close to us, wishing that they attain the same happiness. Most of us are unable to have unconditional love even for relatives and friends at the beginning. But even if our aspirations are contrived, they are still an effective means to help us transcend our limits. Without making these wishes, we would probably never notice how indifferent and narrow-minded we are: we only tend to care about the handful of people who are close to us. How could we ever care about those passersby that are not related to us?

In some situations, we find it harder to unconditionally love those closest to us, given that we tend to have a stronger attachment to them. We expect a lot from them, demanding their total understanding, appreciation, and acceptance. If they fail to follow our wishes, we feel disappointed and hurt. With this mental attitude, to love means to be prepared for upset, and the closer people get, the more problems arise, since expectations are high. To those who are close to us, we do not lack affection but tolerance. When we practice love, we should keep in mind that while every person we meet in life brings meaning to our existence, those who love us make our lives better and more meaningful. This alone merits our gratitude to them.

A bigger challenge is to love strangers or people who are not related to us. It seems rather insincere to simply imagine a crowd and make a general declaration of wishing them happy. But we can extend our love to every single person we meet and let them feel our friendliness. Perhaps there is someone who isn't having a good day, but our friendly gesture relaxes them. This is a good starting point. Then we can wish that their good mood lasts for a while. Minds are connected. If we are filled with kind wishes, others will eventually feel our warmth, even though they may not admit it. If we do not expect reciprocity, we will become more committed to this practice. The inner openness, strength, and tenderness gained from it are the best returns, since they are the true sources of our happiness.

It is extremely difficult to love those we dislike. Consequently, we deal with them last, challenging our mental limit only when we are well-trained and ready. From the initial difficulty of loving ourselves to eventually loving strangers, we have been broadening our mental openness. Until then our indifference does not necessarily come from our lack of ability to love but from our lack of self-confidence in mental openness. In general, a person will not build his or her happiness on the misery of others. This instinct serves as a good basis for us to practice loving-kindness to our enemies, people who have done harm to us, or people we dislike. We can try to have sympathy for their afflictions and test our ability to be tolerant and stay open. People we dislike can always find our weakness at first sight and hit our sensitive spots straightaway. Being with them, therefore, is beneficial to our spiritual practice. As suffering originates from self-attachment, we should first examine ourselves when we suffer because of others. In this regard, enemies are our best teachers. They relentlessly attack what we are most attached to. However difficult it is for us to accept them right now, we will eventually be able to genuinely wish them happiness. Without them, we could never transcend ourselves progressively on the path of loving-kindness.

Finally, we wish that all sentient beings, including animals and beings in other realms of existence, be happy and enjoy the cause of happiness.

May all beings be free of suffering and the cause of suffering—this is the Buddhist concept of compassion. Regardless of our circumstances, we should aspire to live joyfully. This acts as a basis for developing compassion that requires courage and a willingness to bear pain not only for ourselves but also for others. Compared to love, compassion demands more graciousness and strength. What motivates us to suffer willingly is not that we like suffering, but that suffering enables us to let go of pride and see our own weakness. It also allows us to understand others' sadness, worry, and agony. People tend to become aggressive when seeing their own weakness, trying to protect themselves through harshness and ruthlessness. The training of compassion is the other way around—our compassion for ourselves makes us become compassionate toward others. The best protection is neither through making others suffer nor through our evasion of suffering, as this would only work to isolate us and make us colder. Without realizing this, we will keep hurting others and ourselves. Learning to experience pain with an open heart enables us to see other people's suffering with empathy and to gain insight into the cause of suffering. Only then will the wish for all beings to be free of suffering and the cause of suffering have its substance in our minds.

When I was a teenager at Tashi Monastery decades ago, I was very close to a khenpo named Tritsen Gyatsan, who treated me like his own grandson. He often took me with him to perform Dharma activities. Whether he was conferring empowerments or preaching Dharma, he always dissolved into tears as soon as he began speaking about the suffering of all sentient beings. Sometimes we were in a Dharma gathering with a large crowd of devotees. Regardless, he sobbed and wept. I was very young back then, and, being unable to comprehend why Khenpo did this, I thought it was embarrassing and sometimes whispered to him not to do it. Later Khenpo told me that it was his heartfelt pity for all beings at the mere thought of their suffering that brought tears to his eyes. By the time that I grew up to understand Khenpo's compassion, he had long passed away.

Like love, the training of compassion starts with a person or animal that can most easily trigger our sense of compassion. Progressively, we expand our compassion to our relatives and friends, to people who are not related to us, to strangers, to enemies, and finally, to all sentient beings. Whenever anything painful occurs to you, try to be mindful by observing how our emotions shift and how we react to these changes, to sense our own vulnerability, rancor, and fright, and to open our minds as much as possible. Through this process we will come to understand what suffering means to unfortunate people mentioned on TV and radio and in books. Whatever they try to do, we will no longer be appalled. Instead, we will become considerate, and the deeper meaning of humility, tolerance, and gratitude will begin to unfold in our minds.

Whenever we encounter a painful scene, we should not look away immediately but try to feel the pain as much as we can bear and try our best to help. This practice is essential to daily living. In *The Way of the Bodhisattva*, Shantideva teaches in great detail the bodhichitta practice of exchanging oneself with others, which is called *tonglen* in Tibetan and means "giving and receiving." It refers to taking onto ourselves all the pain and giving joy to others. We can practice tonglen through visualization, either for ourselves or for others, in any situation and at any time.

For instance, when you are depressed or exhausted, you can quiet yourself for a moment and mentally focus on your inner feeling, being connected with the self that is utterly wearied under pressure. Then, as you breathe in, you take in all that depression, weariness, and other negative feelings; as you breathe out, you give yourself and others relaxation and vitality. The visualization involved can also be very specific. If your friend cuts his finger accidentally, imagine that he is in front of you and see his cut and feel his pain. Next, as you breathe in, imagine that you breathe in his pain; and as you breathe out, imagine that you send him bandages and painkillers. If you know what he needs most or what relaxes and delights him, such as a cup of tea or a piece of music, you can imagine that you are sending him these things when exhaling. If you do not know what you should give, just imagine what you might need in the same situation and send it to him.

Essential to a compassionate heart is equality. If we think some people are low while others are high, and there is a difference between others and ourselves, we will fail to apprehend the sameness of all beings and their close affinity with us. We should not conflate our sympathy for the unfortunate with a sense of superiority. Otherwise, we will bring them more hurt rather than sharing their pains. Nobody will feel good about being pitied. People in dire situations are more sensitive to equal communication than in any other situations. Therefore, our compassion should be coupled with a strong desire to communicate. What we do is not charitable giving but humane sharing.

On the other hand, it is unwise to be overly humble, too. Neither superiority nor servility facilitates effective communication. Compassion entails sincerely wishing that all beings be happy and free of suffering. Sometimes, excessive compromise and concession make others more aggressive and encourage grasping. They will not become happier or free of afflictions.

Generally, by being compassionate we naturally stay away from anger and hatred. In practice, however, it may actually induce those negative emotions in some people. When people try to save the lives of animals, for example, they may detest those who kill the animals. If you have this kind of tendency, try to watch your own mind. Clearly, you regard yourself as being moral and just and the killers as the opposite. In reality, humans are not easily categorized in such a simple fashion. Every one of us has both positive and negative traits. Without completely removing attachment, none of us can avoid causing harm. To condemn others is like the pot calling the kettle black. Liberation does not depend on whether one is labeled moral or immoral. It transcends labeling. People who practice compassion are the ones who will never abandon anyone, for they believe that all beings have the potential to achieve liberation.

I was often bullied by other kids when I was young due to my inauspicious parentage. Sometimes I became upset, but my anger was only out of childish impulse. It never lasted long, and I never hated anyone. After I started Buddhist practice, I also met people who disparaged the Buddhist teachings or slandered Buddhist teachers. It would be a lie if I said I did not have any negative opinions about those people. But I have never really hated any of them. Instead, I have sympathy for them. While power, wealth, and intelligence are enviable assets in many people's eyes, if they are misused, they become means for evil. Moreover, glory, wealth, and power only last a few decades. Nobody can take these things with them at the time of death. If anything, our clinging to them intensifies our agony.

The cultivation of compassion opens our minds and brings us peace and joy. Joy means that we are grateful for what we have and we rejoice in the fortunes of others. As His Holiness Jigme Phuntsok Rinpoche said, gratitude is the most precious mental quality. People who lack a sense of contentment and seldom feel thankful for their own fortunes will rarely know the joy derived from detachment.

In Tibet, the first step in preliminary Buddhist practice is to reflect and meditate on the preciousness of human existence. Through this practice, we develop heartfelt gratitude and appreciation for what we have. It is not difficult for people to appreciate good things in life, but Buddhist practitioners must remain appreciative and grateful even at difficult times. I have a student whose fiancée suffers from uremia due to kidney failure and has been on dialysis since her twenties. The couple has spent almost two decades in a hospital ward. They neither own a house nor have any savings. Regardless, they live peacefully and never complain, and they wholeheartedly feel lucky for being human and having the good fortune of encountering the Buddhist teachings.

Being appreciative and grateful enables us to do everything with reverence. In our times, a focused and tranquil mind is rare. Joyfulness can help bring us newfound grace and elegance. If we rejoice in others' success, health, virtues, and happiness, we experience sympathetic joy. We will not realize how strong our jealousy is and how easily it can arise in us until we begin to cultivate sympathetic joy. The cultivation of sympathetic joy is seemingly easy but does in fact require tremendous effort. Like love and compassion, we need to go through progressive mind training. Here, whether we start with people closest to us or strangers is not so important. Rather, we should find someone to whom we can most easily say "I am happy for you." Some of us may be more likely to feel jealous of those close to us; others may be the opposite, having no issues with their friends and relatives but feeling reluctant to rejoice in the fortunes of anyone else.

No one is willing to admit their own jealousy, yet few can wholeheartedly rejoice for others. We all know that no benefit can be gained by surrendering to jealousy. Instead, it torments our mind and makes us blind to the merit of others. But jealousy often disguises itself as other emotions that easily deceive us. It can clothe itself in the garb of grievance, for instance.

Although jealousy is good at camouflage, we can still recognize it at once when it arises. But because subconsciously we try to hide our deficiency, we are unwilling to admit it. On the surface, jealousy is about our dissatisfaction with others, while in fact it mirrors our dissatisfaction with ourselves. In this context, jealousy is like a searchlight illuminating our hidden discontent and attachment. If we train ourselves to let go of these negative emotions, we can subdue jealousy and rejoice in others' merit.

Love, compassion, and sympathetic joy all place great emphasis on equality. In the context of Mahayana Buddhism, the practice of equality is not merely out of a demand for justice. It entails an open attitude to embrace and accept all beings without bias, since

Mahayana Buddhism transcends the concepts of self and others, loved ones and strangers, friends and enemies. This mental openness is called the "boundless quality of impartiality" in Buddhism. Traditionally, the mind training in the four boundless qualities starts with impartiality. It is the starting point and foundation of love and compassion. As Patrul Rinpoche says in his *Words of My Perfect Teacher*, impartiality is like inviting everybody to a banquet where nobody will be rejected.

The four boundless qualities, while being separately discussed for easier understanding, are essentially inseparable and interwoven. We call these qualities boundless because the beings these qualities benefit are vast and infinite, and the benefit they bring is immeasurable. Without impartiality, the other three of the four boundless qualities will lack true altruism and fail to be boundless; and without the other three, impartiality becomes apathy and indifference.

With a mind supported by the four boundless qualities, we wish all sentient beings to attain complete enlightenment, to be happy and free of suffering. This altruistic wish is called bodhichitta in aspiration. We can aspire to attain enlightenment ourselves first before helping others achieve the same; or to be liberated from cyclic existence together with all sentient beings; or to be like the great bodhisattvas Samantabhadra and Kshitigarbha, who vow not to attain complete enlightenment until all sentient beings have become buddhas. The scope of our aspirations can be either big or small, depending on our individual conditions and capacities, but they are of no difference in terms of quality. Any honest aspiration driven by the genuine desire for the liberation of all sentient beings deserves our admiration. It is not necessary for us to pursue the ultimate vast attitude only for the sake of being a qualified Mahayana bodhisattva.

After we have generated bodhichitta in aspiration, it is conceivable that we may still be selfish and unwise, and our journey remains long before we reach enlightenment. Our actions and speech must therefore rely on the powerful means of the six transcendent perfections to make our aspirations come true. The practice of the six transcendent perfections is called bodhichitta in action, which comprises generosity, discipline, patience, diligence, concentration, and wisdom.

Together, bodhichitta in aspiration and bodhichitta in action are termed *relative bodhichitta*. Through long-term training in relative bodhichitta to accumulate merit and wisdom, we eventually arrive at direct insight into the uncontrived nature of all phenomena that is called *absolute bodhichitta*. Absolute bodhichitta can only be realized through spiritual practice, whereas relative bodhichitta are generated through rituals by which we take the bodhisattva vow and are strengthened through various acts of the six transcendent perfections. While beginners' relative bodhichitta is undoubtedly contrived, persistent mind training will eventually make uncontrived bodhichitta manifest naturally.

In Sanskrit, the six transcendent perfections are called *paramitas* meaning "to the other shore." Crossing over to the other shore is a metaphor for transcending the narrow view of dualism to reach enlightenment through the practice of six transcendent perfections. The scope of the six transcendent perfections is extensive, as expounded by Shantideva in his *Way of the Bodhisattva* and by the seventh-century Indian scholar Chandrakirti in his *Entering the Middle Way*. What I am going to explain only concerns their basic meanings. The six transcendent perfections are not the code of conduct for a good Buddhist, nor are they mandatory rules imposed on practitioners. For Mahayana practitioners, every act motivated by bodhichitta is viewed as an effective means for fulfilling the bodhisattva aspiration.

When we practice giving to the weak and needy, we should not do it out of fear of losing face. To do good deeds out of religious or philosophical intent does not accord with the Buddhist teachings either. The essence of giving, from the Buddhist perspective, is to let go of our own desire and attachment. Regardless of the value of things given, if we only give away what we no longer need or cherish, the act of giving is impure in light of its motivation.

Since we let go of attachment and worldly desire through giving, it is not the same as charity. Neither should we take pride, feel complacent, or worry about what might be the result of our giving. The very idea of giving is to offer others what we have. If we intentionally look for opportunities to give or to amass things for the purpose of giving, giving in itself becomes a kind of attachment, which is against the true spirit of giving. In its most sublime form, giving means that we can give away anything we have at any time and do not desire what we do not have. While this concerns material giving, the same principle applies to giving Dharma and giving protection from fear.

Buddhist precepts often are mistaken for restrictions that prohibit Buddhists from doing certain things. In reality, Buddhist precepts are not so rigid and harsh. They refer to proper behaviors, namely, doing the right things at the right time in order not to harm any being. Examining our speech and bodily actions, we may find we often do wrong things at the wrong time. Out of his great compassion, the Buddha teaches us self-discipline in order to help us live in harmony with ourselves, with others, and with the environment. Consequently, we no longer have to suffer due to ineptness. Our present way of life can only make buddhas and bodhisattvas laugh. Jigme Lingpa once said that discipline is for us to avoid embarrassment in front of buddhas and bodhisattvas.

We must maintain mindfulness to avoid rash judgment and impulsive reactions in any situation. This is precisely the core of patience, which allows us to adapt to any circumstance and to be receptive to every possibility. The mind of a Mahayana practitioner is always open. It never hopes or averts, and thus has no fear and frustration; it is ever pliable and expansive, and thus always ready to embrace all situations with courage.

Through generosity, we let go of clinging. As we become less attached, our actions will be less likely to cause harm—this is discipline. We are no longer susceptible to anger and hatred—this is patience. These practices bring about changes that further inspire and encourage us, leading us to the next stage of the bodhisattva practice prompted by both perseverance and joy. Our practice is no longer motivated by obligation. We are intrigued and amazed by our creativity and our potential to change, and we want to explore more. If our lives are too cumbersome to allow us to pursue this quest, we will be more than happy to simplify them. If this quest requires us to dedicate entire lifetimes to it, we will be more than willing to do so. We will not be frustrated and impatient, no matter how long and winding the journey appears to be—this is diligence.

Concentration refers to refraining from distraction. Usually, without the practice of meditation, it is difficult to bring the mind under control. Our minds are scattered and under constant influence of outer phenomena. Therefore, to maintain concentration without a spiritual practice is nearly impossible amid various distractions. It is for this reason that beginners should stay away from hustle and bustle and stay in places that are suitable for generating concentration. Practitioners of past generations have repeatedly lauded the supreme merit of secluded places. Ultimately, if we are mindful and remain undistracted, anything we do is the practice of concentration.

Wisdom realizing emptiness is called *prajna paramita* in Sanskrit and is beyond conceptual elaboration. Its direct experience is something close to a mental state of extreme openness, expansiveness, clarity, pliability, and detachment. One who achieves this does not hope for what is to come, nor resist what is coming, nor cling to what has gone. Instead, they embrace all possibilities. With an open and lucid mind dedicated to cultivating the virtues of generosity, discipline, patience, diligence, and concentration, they will eventually experience all-pervasive emptiness, the essence of universal phenomena.

After we have generated bodhichitta, we might still hope that we have an exit strategy if things turn sour. This is not surprising. Without the presumption of an exit, we would probably never venture to do anything. Nonetheless, time only goes in one direction, and life travels like a river without return. Whatever has happened can never be reversed, and there is no door for us to retreat through. The bodhisattva vow enables us to defeat our habitual self-deception.

If we truly believe that all sentient beings in samsara have the same innate nature as buddhas, we will realize that, when it comes to our relationship with other beings, we have never had any choice but to accept that they are inseparable from us. The bodhisattva vow is not a fabrication out of nothing but a reflection of this reality. The difference between before and after taking the bodhisattva vow is our own mental attitude: we no longer regard ourselves as separate from others and no longer believe ourselves separable from others. This realization is so striking and vivid that it will ever inspire the nascent bodhichitta to grow in us. Bodhichitta is like a seed, and the related vows and precepts are like soil, sun, and rain that shelter and stimulate the seed to take root, sprout, and grow.

Bodhichitta is such an elemental part of our human experience that we often forget that it requires diligent training to cultivate. Nevertheless, it is the root of Mahayana practice. Whenever people ask me how long we should cultivate bodhichitta, my answer is "life after life."

The One Who Inspires

As we take refuge in the Three Jewels, we hear, contemplate, and practice the Buddhist teachings, making efforts in generating and developing both renunciation and bodhichitta and trying to understand the view of emptiness. The path appears to unfold smoothly, but one issue always stands before us: How do we navigate our relationship with our spiritual teachers?

It seems impossible for us to find a path to liberation without the guidance of an authentic teacher. The fact that we remain deluded in this painful cyclic existence serves as evidence: searching alone, we are like blind men in the middle of a deserted plain. The wisdom of the Buddha is a beacon that allows us to see in the long dark nights of our quest for liberation. When the Buddha achieved complete enlightenment in India's Bodh Gaya some twenty-five hundred years ago, we were wandering somewhere else in samsara and missed the chance to follow him. And we have missed the chance of liberation again and again since then, due to our arrogance, bias, obstinacy, clinging, and cowardice. Nevertheless, there is someone out there waiting for endless nights to lighten our path with Buddhist wisdom. If we miss them again, they say they will wait until the day when we finally meet them. Such is the compassion of a spiritual teacher.

A spiritual teacher is called a *lama* in Tibetan, a term similar to *guru* in Sanskrit. When we start to turn our minds inward instead of looking outward, we are ready to meet our spiritual teachers. We can certainly read, contemplate, or practice according to written instructions on our own. But we have long been used to interpreting words subjectively, and our thinking is constrained by self-centeredness.

Without the aid of our teachers, we will not be able to achieve direct experience and complete realization of the innate nature of the mind. Spiritual teachers provoke thinking and transmit suitable methods of practice. Thus they are essential on our spiritual path. If a teacher is the one who is spiritually accomplished, they can assist the student in progressing not only properly but also quickly and directly to bring about realization. Shakyamuni Buddha once said that no buddha of the past attained Buddhahood without the guidance of authentic teachers. And it is with the help of their teachers that all the one thousand buddhas in the Fortunate Aeon to which we belong have achieved or will achieve complete enlightenment. If we had the same insight as that of a buddha, we would understand the central significance of having a spiritual teacher.

The fourteenth-century Tibetan Buddhist text *The Wish-Fulfilling Treasure* composed by the omniscient Longchenpa says that it is through the blessing of a qualified master that a practitioner develops the merit and wisdom necessary for attaining enlightenment. Longchenpa, who was the abbot of Samye Monastery, Tibet's first Buddhist monastery, was one of the most brilliant masters of the Nyingma school, and is regarded as an earthly manifestation of Manjushri, the Bodhisattva of Wisdom.

An authentic and qualified spiritual teacher is a necessity for Buddhist practitioners, since aspirations alone are not sufficient to transcend birth and death on the path to spiritual realization. To liberate ourselves from samsara, we need to learn from teachers what to do and what to avoid in accordance with the karmic law of cause and effect, as well as how to watch our minds and actions carefully. Spiritual teachers are also the field of merit for us to accumulate merit and wisdom quickly and effectively. Their blessings are the most powerful means to save beings from the pain of samsara. Relying on them is the quickest way to help us deepen faith, compassion, and wisdom. On the path to enlightenment, nothing else is better than a spiritual teacher acting as our guiding light.

Undoubtedly, we earnestly hope to learn Dharma and attain liberation. Otherwise, we would neither have chosen this path, which is particularly difficult to traverse in an age filled with temptations and doubts, nor would we willingly follow our spiritual teachers. Yet we often underestimate the tricky and stubborn side of our ego and its ability to resort to every possible means of self-defense. This ego might materialize at any time to mar our connections with our teachers. Why is our selfish ego so threatened by authentic spiritual teachers?

Let us first look at what a student will do in the Tibetan tradition when he meets a teacher. Normally, he will make an offering as well as bow to the teacher. This is not merely an act of politeness and respect but carries a much deeper meaning. Offerings include practice, service, and material objects. Among the three, the most valuable is the offering of practice consisting of putting whatever the teacher teaches into practice with determination and diligence. His Holiness Jigme Phuntsok Rinpoche often stressed that it is largely through Dharma practice that one makes a positive connection with him, and the offering of practice pleases him the most. This is because it is through the practice of Buddhadharma that we eradicate our attachment to ego, to a self.

Authentic teachers are not interested in material things, but material things are often objects of fixation in this world. If a student gives food, goods, or money to his teacher—objects of his attachment—it signifies their willingness to let go of clinging and to follow the teacher. Not only do material offerings help subdue attachment to a self, but they are also a convenient means to accumulate wisdom and merit.

Any kind of material offering to a teacher can be good—the kind or amount given is not of central significance. The truth is that the merit of offering hinges on motivation. If you are motivated by ostentation, you will not necessarily gain much merit even if your offering is abundant. On the other hand, as His Holiness Jigme Phuntsok

Rinpoche once said, while the amount that a student offers is not essential, it can still be a good reference point to gauge his devotion to the teacher. Without faith, one would not be inclined to make any material offerings to the teacher and the Three Jewels. But with faith, devotion, and pure motivation, one can accumulate great merit through making offerings, regardless of the amount that is offered.

During the time of the Buddha, there was an old homeless woman who often saw the king, prince, and other people making offerings to the Buddha and his disciples. She, too, hoped to make an offering as they did. One day, she received a copper coin after having begged for the entire day. She wanted to buy some offering oil with the coin, but found that she could not afford to buy the oil for even a single oil lamp. Out of mercy, the oil vendor gave her some oil for free. Joyfully, she went to a temple and made a light offering. While doing so, she also made a wish: "I have nothing other than lighting this lamp to offer. But by the merit of this offering, I hope to attain wisdom one day. When that day comes, may I have the ability to help all sentient beings to dispel the darkness in their minds and guide them to attain enlightenment."

That night, all but one lamp went out. The lamp that remained burning till daybreak was the one offered by the old homeless woman. Not only was the oil in the lamp not reduced, but the wick also stayed new. Maudgalyayana, who possessed the greatest supernatural powers among all the Buddha's disciples, came to take care of the offering lamps at daybreak. He wanted to extinguish the lamp so that he could light it again when the Buddha gave teachings at night. But however hard he tried, he could not extinguish it. Hearing this, the Buddha came to Maudgalyayana and said, "You will never be able to extinguish the light of this lamp. Even if you poured over it all the water from the world's oceans, rivers, and lakes, it would continue burning simply because it was offered with a pure intent, the aspiration for the ultimate liberation of all beings." At that moment the old woman arrived, and the Buddha prophesized that she would one day attain supreme Buddhahood under a name meaning "the Lamp Buddha."

Evidently, with pure motivation, even the smallest offering can accumulate extraordinary merit. According to some Buddhist sutras and commentarial texts, any delightful scene we see, such as a babbling stream or wild flowers, can be offered through visualization as a feast to the eyes of our spiritual teachers. Doing so also brings us inconceivable merit.

The offering of service is essentially to do whatever our spiritual teachers require us to do. Since an authentic teacher's every action is for the benefit of all sentient beings and in accordance with the Buddhist teachings, our assistance to that teacher indirectly benefits all beings and protects the Dharma. Moreover, our rejoicing in teachers' activities and accomplishments acts like tiny drops joining a vast ocean, allowing us to share the ocean-like merit of the teachers. So, whatever we do for our teachers generates both wisdom and merit, which are essential to the realization of emptiness as well as to the attainment of complete enlightenment.

Whenever I got an opportunity to serve my root lama His Holiness Jigme Phuntsok Rinpoche, I was always happy. After His Holiness passed away, one day at daybreak, I dreamed that I was on retreat. To my surprise, His Holiness, whom I missed dearly, came to the front of the cave where I was staying. I was ecstatic and went out to greet him. Smiling, His Holiness sat down on a Tibetan-style rug. Afraid that the rock behind him might hurt his head and back, I went inside to fetch a woolen blanket to use as a cushion. I was both happy and nervous, and I tried and tried but could not fold the blanket into a proper shape. I kept trying until I woke up, and the tremendous joy of seeing and serving His Holiness lingered. Offerings can also be categorized by the three kinds of offerings of body, speech, and mind. A student's Dharma practice is the offering of practice through body, speech, and mind. Their offering of service is through body and speech. And their rejoicing in their teachers' acts is through their mind. Whichever way we offer, it helps deepen our faith and loosen our grasp on the self.

The Tibetan-style prostration where one's limbs and head completely touch the ground demands deep humility, which includes the shedding of pride and the acceptance of any situation. Through prostration one accumulates tremendous merit and wisdom. The sutras say that on top of the Buddha's head was a crown made of flesh that was round and circled clockwise. This is one of the thirty-two major marks of the Buddha and is the result of the devotion and homage he paid to his spiritual teachers.

So, by making offerings and performing prostrations to a spiritual teacher, one becomes ready to let go of one's ego, mentally preparing to be a student of that teacher. It is for this reason that our ego resists teachers—in front of them, it has no foothold.

Let us turn now to ourselves: what kind of attitude do we usually have when meeting a teacher? First, we might initially have a stereotypical image of a teacher in mind before actually meeting them. We might expect them to look sagely, fine, noble, dignified, and gracious. We might expect them to be able to fulfill our needs and wishes, giving us solace and help whenever needed. We might even expect them to display supernatural abilities from time to time so that we will not become bored or lose patience on the path. Then, when we go to see the teacher, if they fail to meet our preconceived ideas and expectations, we may be disappointed and begin to doubt whether they possess authentic wisdom and merit.

After meeting, not everyone will be immediately sure that they should form a bond with the teacher. It is necessary to examine the teacher carefully before becoming committed to them through receiving empowerments and teachings. A spiritual teacher is our paramount source of refuge in cyclic existence. We are going to place our trust in the teacher for all our future lives. It is they who will teach us what to do and what to avoid on the spiritual path. Without careful examination, we might end up with an unqualified teacher and fall further into the cycle of samsaric suffering.

To examine teachers carefully is of particular importance on the tantric path because, once established, the formal relationship between a teacher and a student cannot be destroyed. Otherwise, the tantric vow will be transgressed or even broken, and the related causal effects will be extremely deleterious. Patrul Rinpoche's *Words of My Perfect Teacher* elucidates clearly how to discern an authentic teacher. Although in the degenerate age we can rarely find a spiritual teacher who possesses all the qualities described in the sutras and tantras, a qualified teacher should at least meet the following criteria: they have true bodhichitta; they have learned and mastered various teachings and practices in order to transmit complete sets of realization methods suitable for students; and they are pure observers of received vows and precepts, including the commitments of tantric practice, which are called *samaya*s in Sanskrit.

When it comes to examining a vajra teacher, the teacher's keeping of samayas is paramount. *Vajra* is not a title like khenpo, tulku, or rinpoche. It indicates a solemn and specific commitment between a tantric teacher and a student. When a tantric teacher bestows a tantric empowerment, gives a tantric teaching, and transmits a pith instruction to you, this teacher has formed a special bond with you and becomes your vajra teacher. If the teacher transgresses the tantric vow, they have broken the tantric lineage of the Dharma and are therefore no longer qualified to confer on you any empowerment and teaching. Some people are fastidious about everyday trivialities like what to eat and how to dress. But when it comes to choosing a spiritual teacher, they are sometimes careless, as if anyone could be their spiritual teacher.

The kinds of teachers one meets depends on one's attitude and karmic connection with the teachers. This is also dependent on collective karma in the era to which they belong. Shakyamuni manifested as the Buddha at his time. Following his nirvana, beings—due to their dwindling fortunes—could only see buddhas manifest as arhats, and then *panditas*, which is a Sanskrit word meaning "learned masters." Now that we are in the degenerate age, our minds and eyes only let us see ordinary people, so buddhas manifest as commoners in this world to benefit us. For each individual, meeting a kind and wise teacher in this lifetime requires merit gathered over many lifetimes. And if one's attitude and motivation are not pure, they will be blind to the qualities of a spiritual teacher, even if the teacher is a real buddha. In this respect, to examine a teacher is essentially about examining our own minds. That is, what kind of intent we have when we seek out a teacher. Do we aim for spiritual liberation or for something else? And if we strive for spiritual liberation, do we aim for our individual liberation from cyclic existence or for the liberation of all sentient beings? Do we aim for the knowledge and realization of the absolute truth of universal phenomena, or do we only intend to experience certain meditative states or acquire new identities?

If you have a pure attitude, you will recognize a buddha's embodiment even if they appear as an ordinary person in front of you; if you do not have the right mental attitude, no matter how qualified a spiritual teacher is, you remain blind to their virtues. Devadatta and Sunakshatra were the Buddha's cousins, who had been following the Buddha for several decades. However, both of them thought that they were more spiritually accomplished than the Buddha. The actual manifestation of buddhas in this world is subject to the collective karma of beings, whereas your own ability to identify your teacher as a real buddha depends entirely on your own merit and wisdom.

With regard to how one should examine a spiritual teacher, *The Words of My Perfect Teacher* offers this specific counsel:

In the first place, you should take care to check the teacher. Before becoming committed to him through empowerments and teachings, you should examine him with care. Should you find that he has all the characteristics of a teacher, follow him. If some of them are lacking, do not follow him. But, from the moment you start to follow him, learn to have faith in him and see him with pure perception, thinking only of his virtues and seeing whatever he does as positive. Looking for flaws in him will only bring you inconceivable ills.

In addition, it is paramount that your mind be closely connected with the mind of your teachers. Following a spiritual teacher is called *lama la tenpa* in Tibetan. *Tenpa* means to follow, to unconditionally rely on, and to firmly believe that by doing so liberation will be attained. Each of us has different connections with our teachers. Some, when simply hearing the name of the teacher or meeting them for the first time, will feel a strong physical and emotional reaction. For instance, merely hearing the name of the translator Marpa was enough to arouse in Milarepa an extraordinary faith from the very depth of his being, even though he had never seen Marpa before. Others develop trust and faith over time through regular contact and learning. Some have the chance to stay at the side of their teachers over a long period, as in the case of Lama Ösel, who had followed Mipham Rinpoche and been his attendant for thirty-seven years until Mipham Rinpoche's passing. Others have to leave their teachers shortly after having received teachings from them. Atisha had more than one hundred teachers. Sudhana, a youth from ancient India, learned from many spiritual teachers through a lengthy pilgrimage to various places. In a nutshell, to follow a teacher does not depend on whether one is physically near to or far from the teacher. If one is mentally connected with the teacher, grasps their teachings, integrates the teachings with their own mind, and has heartfelt gratitude for the teacher's virtues and kindness, they are able to obtain never-ending blessings of the teacher. This constitutes the very essence of following a spiritual teacher: relying on them to reach liberation.

There is a difference between keeping one's distance from a teacher prior to close examination of them and becoming disappointed with a teacher due to preconceived ideas about what a teacher should be like. You should consider whether you examine the teacher without bias or whether you merely feel that the teacher differs from what you fondly hoped for or imagined. Once in a while, a teacher will deliberately surprise you or even disappoint you in order to challenge your mental openness. If you hope to see an awe-inspiring teacher, they may show you their ill-mannered side; if you think a teacher should be gentle and soft-spoken, they may appear stern and critical; if you believe a teacher should look like an immortal sage, they may burp, pick their teeth, fall ill, and grow old just like anybody else.

When Milarepa, who desired to attain Buddhahood in one lifetime, met his future teacher Marpa for the first time, Marpa was plowing the field looking like a common farmer. When the well-known pandita Naropa met Tilopa, a homeless person whom the locals thought was mad, but who was a great mahasiddha in disguise, Tilopa was eating fish in a shack. When Sadaprarudita finally met Dharmodgata after overcoming many hardships, Dharmodgata was enjoying pleasures in a palace. Examples like these are too numerous to count.

It seems that all teachers deploy the same tactics. They challenge your preconceptions right from the start so that you feel lost and perplexed, wondering how deluded and ridiculous your biased thinking is—especially toward the one whom you seek out to be your spiritual teacher. My late uncle Lorung Tanpa loved to tell a story from his childhood. When his father, my maternal grandfather, passed away, the family invited the famous Tulku Sonam Gyatso home to perform transference rituals for him. Surprisingly, Tulku went straight to sleep after having a good meal upon arrival. This made my uncle worried. Tulku did not wake up till the next day at noon. Then he smiled and said, "I'd better hurry to recite some texts. Otherwise, this boy will think I do nothing other than eat his food."

Hearing this, my uncle was both astounded and ashamed, and an overwhelming sense of faith in Tulku dawned on him.

If whatever the teacher has done has not scared you away, it might be the first time that you have managed to resist your ego's cajolery, not being enticed away by it. Unhappy with the failure, your proud and cunning ego will refuse to submit and start playing new tricks. "Well done," it will flatter you. "You must have such good fortune to be a student of this important person. How wise you are indeed, much wiser than those common people and nobler than any Buddhists of other traditions. You are one of a kind, supremely capable. You are such a fit vessel for Buddhist learning." Such sweet talk pleases you and makes you feel inflated, unaware that this is just the ego's usual tricks.

At your ego's instigation, you are busy playing your new role. In front of non-Buddhists, you act as a Buddhist; in front of Buddhists, you act as an accomplished Buddhist; and in front of your teacher, you act as a devoted and obedient disciple. Sometimes you play the role consciously, but most of the time you play it subconsciously. In other words, you perceive yourself as a Buddhist, but in reality you are only playing. You change your diet, lapse into Buddhist jargon, and live a different routine. You perform regular incense offerings, prostrations, and animal life-release, spending money and efforts on religious activities and charity. What truly matters, though, is your motivation. What really inspires your action—to prove to others you have a Buddhist identity or to make yourself feel good as you are on a path well-acknowledged by others or to explore the true nature of your mind? The eighty-four thousand methods of Dharma taught by the Buddha all lead to liberation. No matter which method you practice, you must take it to heart and really apply it in order to transform your deluded mind. If your practice is only a cosmetic measure, you will never succeed in real terms.

You hear your ego saying, "The teacher is crucial to one's liberation. You must make a good impression." So, you work hard in order to demonstrate your best side to your teacher, vying for their attention and favor. In sutras and tantras, there are detailed instructions regarding how students should behave, such as being gentle, unassuming, and respectful instead of being rude, pompous, and ostentatious. These good manners usually require deliberate imitations before they become cultivated personal qualities. Therefore, provided one is respectful and devoted, it is acceptable if they are somewhat contrived in front of the teacher. I have a student who always behaves with extreme reverence and awe. His manner appears so dramatic that it often makes others laugh. Although as his teacher, I myself do not have much virtue and merit, his sincerity and devotion gain him vast merit. So I often rejoice in his acts. If such behavior, however, is meant to show that you are more polite, graceful, educated, and open-minded than other students in order to be treated favorably by your teacher, it will be hard for you to connect your mind with your teacher's mind.

The story of Kongpo Ben in *The Words of My Perfect Teacher* may be enlightening. Once, in the province of Kongpo, there lived a simple-minded man named Ben. He made a journey to Lhasa to see Jowo Rinpoche, the famous statue of the Buddha at the Jokhang Temple. When he arrived in front of the statue, there was no caretaker or anyone else nearby. He was tired and hungry. Seeing *torma* (Tibetan offering cakes) and the butter lamps in front of it, he imagined that Jowo Rinpoche must dip pieces of the offering cakes in the melted butter of the lamps and eat them. The wicks were burning in the lamps, he supposed, to keep the butter liquid.

"I think I'd better eat some, like Jowo Rinpoche does," he thought to himself, and, dunking a piece of dough from the torma into the butter, he ate it. Then he looked at the smiling face of the Jowo. "What a nice lama you are," he said. "Even when dogs come and steal the food you've been offered, you smile; when the draft makes your lamps sputter, you still keep smiling. Here, I'll leave you my boots. Please look after them for me while I walk around you." He took off his boots and put them up in front of the statue. While he was walking around the pathway that circles the temple, the caretaker returned and saw the boots. He was about to throw them out when the statue started to speak: "Don't throw those boots away. Kongpo Ben has entrusted them to me."

Ben eventually came back and took his boots. "You really are what they call a good lama!" he said to the statue. "Next year, why don't you come and visit us. I'll cook you a nice meal and brew you up some nice old barley beer." The Jowo replied, "I'll come."

After his return, Ben told his wife, "I've invited Jowo Rinpoche. I am not sure exactly when he's coming, though. So, don't forget to keep an eye out for him." A year went by. One day, as Ben's wife was drawing water from a river, a clear reflection of Jowo Rinpoche appeared in the water. She ran home and told her husband, "There's something down in the river. I wonder if it's the person you invited."

Ben rushed down to the river and saw Jowo Rinpoche shining in the water. Thinking that he must have fallen into the river, Ben jumped in after him. As he grabbed at the image, he found that he could actually hold it and bring it along with him.

For Ben, the statue of the Jowo Buddha looked like the real Buddha himself. He did not think that Jowo Rinpoche was an ancient Indian who once lived some thousand kilometers away, but a lama who was present and with whom he could talk. This lama was not a god or fairy, who flew around in the sky and lived without the need to eat. Neither was the torma only for display in front of the statue. This lama could encounter rain and wind and could accidentally fall into the water and need to be rescued. Ben must have wholeheartedly revered and admired Jowo Rinpoche. The reason he revered and admired him was not because Jowo Rinpoche had fame and possessed miraculous power, but because he was a good lama who always smiled even when dogs stole his torma and a draft sputtered the offering butter lamps. In Ben's mind, there was no room for presumptions. He did not try to act as a devotee, supposing what he was meant to do and avoid doing in front of a lama—he knew none of these things. All he did was enter into the presence of his lama, hoping to get close to him.

Each of us reacts differently when in the presence of our teachers. Some of us may be relaxed, others reserved; some may be courtly, others abrupt. In times past, whenever my spiritual brothers and I went to see His Holiness Jigme Phuntsok Rinpoche, we would pace at the doorway for a long time, feeling extremely awkward. As none of us dared to enter the room first, we often had to use dice to decide who should be the first to enter. But however you may feel, being connected with your teacher will become easier if you remain open and honest.

His Holiness Jigme Phuntsok Rinpoche often spoke of his early years of Buddhist study under Thubga Rinpoche, whom he greatly revered. Although he was eager to be in the presence of Thubga Rinpoche, he would never dare to approach him without being called over. He often gazed at his lama's small house from a distance, hoping to catch sight of him. If Thubga Rinpoche inadvertently spotted him and called him over, he would be elated.

Another story often told by His Holiness Jigme Phuntsok Rinpoche was about his first meeting with Pema Siddhi Rinpoche, who was regarded as the true embodiment of Avalokiteshvara, the Bodhisattva of compassion. Prior to meeting Pema Siddhi Rinpoche, His Holiness Jigme Phuntsok Rinpoche assumed that Rinpoche would be finely dressed and have a regal look. However, what he saw was an old man no different from a commoner. He thought something was wrong with his eyes, so he rubbed them and looked again. But the lama was still the same simple, gentle old man. His Holiness Jigme Phuntsok Rinpoche said to himself, "It must be my karmic obscurations that hinder me from seeing the real manifestation of Avalokiteshvara." He closed his eyes, repenting and praying fervently, while his confidence in Rinpoche's being Avalokiteshvara never faltered for even a second. His Holiness Jigme Phuntso

Rinpoche's pure perception pleased Rinpoche greatly. Praising him, Pema Siddhi Rinpoche said to his disciples, "Today a great bodhisattva under Thugba Rinpoche has joined our gathering. His coming will multiply the merit of our mantra recitations. How fortunate we are to have him! I always ask you to count your recitation strictly. But today is a rare occasion. Let us add some extra recitations." As soon as he said this, he started to move forward several prayer beads in his rosary string (one bead in the string may represent one hundred or one thousand mantra recitations). His Holiness Jigme Phuntsok Rinpoche often used this story to teach his students: "We may not be able to see our lamas being the embodiments of buddhas or bodhisattvas due to our insufficient merit and limited conditions. As long as we do not follow our deluded thoughts but genuinely repent our karmic obscurations, our lamas will be delighted and their compassionate blessings will pour into our minds."

As the saying goes, a thousand rivers have a thousand reflections of the moon. While the moon in the sky is the very same moon, its reflection in different rivers will vary. The brilliance and clarity of the moon's reflection depends on the state of the river. The mind of a teacher is like the brilliant moon in the sky, and the mental quality of a student is like a river. The stiller and purer the student's mind is, the brighter and clearer the moon's reflection in it will become; the murkier and the more turbulent the mind is, the more fragmented and obscured the moon's reflection will be. Meanwhile, as long as there is water in the river, there will always be a reflection of the moon regardless of whether the water is clear or murky. Therefore, you should not think that you are the only one who is connected with your teacher. Neither should you be troubled by the fact that others have a close connection with your teacher—this will not diminish the power of your connection. Sometimes we might become annoyed by fellow students' relationship with our teacher and even try to prevent our teacher from reaching out to these students. This self-centeredness often constitutes an obstacle to our spiritual progress, since what we perceive as faith is, in effect, attachment. It hinders not only our relationship with fellow students but also our relationship with our teacher. Slowly, we find it harder and harder to reach the mind of the teacher.

Vast, open, and clear faith repels neither spiritual friends nor any other qualified teachers. If you can keep the promise to never abandon your present teacher, you can always go meet and follow other teachers who have a connection with you. A student does not have to follow just one teacher. A spiritual teacher is not the property of an individual student, nor is a student the property of an individual teacher. Some practitioners whose faith is clear and pure may follow many teachers because of their connections with them and the necessity to engage in different practices. Doing so does not undermine the student's faith in any of their teachers or create conflict. Whether it is better for you to follow one or several teachers depends on the strength of your faith. If you desert your previous teacher after meeting a new one, you have effectively deserted all teachers and will lose all of their blessings.

Three practitioners once came to Khyentse Yeshi Dorje for a particular tantric initiation. Khyentse Yeshi Dorje is regarded as the mind emanation of Jigme Lingpa. He told them that they could receive the initiation only if they agreed to abandon their existing teacher. Since it was a very special initiation, two practitioners finally agreed to this request. The one who refused was called Wo're. He said, "My teacher does not have any fault. I will not even pretend to abandon him by paying you lip service." He was then expelled from the initiation gathering. However, when the dejected Wo're was on his way back, Khyentse Yeshi Dorje sent someone to fetch him. The great master extolled him in public: "We should all be like Wo're and follow our lamas." Then Khyentse Yeshi Dorje had the other two practitioners expelled from the monastery. Subsequently, Wo're stayed for many years at the side of Khyentse Yeshi Dorje, who deemed him "an accomplished being no different from me."

BUSINESS REPLY MAIL
FIRST-CLASS MAIL   PERMIT NO. 1100   SOMERVILLE, MA

POSTAGE WILL BE PAID BY ADDRESSEE

WISDOM PUBLICATIONS
199 ELM ST
SOMERVILLE MA 02144-9908

Wisdom

WISDOM PUBLICATIONS

Please fill out and return this card if you would like to receive our catalogue and special offers. The postage is already paid!

NAME

ADDRESS

CITY / STATE / ZIP / COUNTRY

EMAIL

Sign up for our newsletter and special offers at wisdompubs.org

Wisdom Publications is a non-profit charitable organization.

In the eyes of devoted students like us, nothing is more righteous than pleasing our teachers. We do whatever we can to honor our teachers. This intent is undoubtedly pure. However, sometimes our wish to honor our teachers can become an excuse for being stubborn, narrow, and intolerant to other fellow students, especially if we believe that what we do is absolutely right. Actually, it is vital to maintain respect and harmony among spiritual friends in general and vajra spiritual friends in particular. Vajra spiritual friends are our companions on the path to Buddhahood. Conflicts among them are upsetting to teachers, casting obstacles to their Dharma transmissions and their lifespans. If we look into it, the root of our problem is still our attachment to a self, which can make a fool of us at any time and turn our best intentions into obstacles.

Of the fourteen root tantric vows defined in the *Kalachakra Tantra*, three concern vajra teachers: Do not disturb the minds of our vajra teachers; do not transgress teachers' injunctions; and do not fault vajra brothers and sisters because of anger. The third one, in particular, is often neglected. Although it is well understood that a vajra teacher is a critical karmic object of one's actions, few are aware that tensions and conflicts among vajra students will harm their vajra teachers. In this context, vajra spiritual friends are critical karmic objects as well.

When we have the chance to work with our vajra spiritual friends in assisting our teachers and spreading Buddhism, we should cherish this opportunity and rejoice in others' good intentions and deeds. If we have different thoughts, we should resort to friendly communication. Sometimes, in order to help others fulfill their kind wishes, we do not have to insist on our ways of doing things or doing what we regard as right or positive. Neither do we have to insist on perfection, as it is already perfect if all of us, through doing things together, can subdue individual afflictions and enhance joy and confidence. His Holiness Jigme Phuntsok Rinpoche advised his students not to disturb other people's minds. The omniscient Longchenpa advised practitioners that the best offering to spiritual teachers is to follow what they say. We who are stubborn and unwise with regard to cause and effect should always remember these pieces of advice, just as it is said in the common ending of sutras that "all who heard what the Buddha had said sincerely rejoiced, believing, accepting, honoring, and practicing it."

According to the *Longchen Nyingthig*, a terma cycle revealed by Jigme Lingpa in the eighteenth century that provides a comprehensive explanation of the Great Perfection, one's mind will merge completely with the teacher's mind and the two will become one. This is possible if the student regards the teacher as a real buddha and prays to him with complete faith and fervent devotion, provided the teacher in question is a realized being whose lineage is unstained. By the power of his blessings alone, realization will take place. When His Holiness Jigme Phuntsok Rinpoche was fifteen years old, he prayed to Mipham Rinpoche fervently with peerless confidence in the Great Perfection. Each time he recited one hundred times the prayer to Mipham Rinpoche, he would go through Mipham Rinpoche's pith instruction on the Great Perfection, *Directly Pointing to the Nature of the Mind*. After one million recitations of the prayer and ten thousand sessions of careful study and contemplation of *Directly Pointing to the Nature of the Mind*, His Holiness attained realization of the Great Perfection.

That being said, you are wrong if you think that you do not have to worry anymore provided you let your teacher decide everything for you. Perhaps you simply do not want to be responsible for yourself. During our endless lives in cyclical existence, we have seen a lot and suffered a lot; yet our memories are short-lived. Life after life, we go on living muddle-headedly, twisted and entangled in the same game without knowing it. Shakyamuni said, "I preach the way of liberation to you, but you are the master of your own liberation." If you do not make any effort but hope your teacher will deliver you to the Pure Land like casting a stone, your wishful thinking will surely fail you.

Even if your teacher is immensely powerful and his compassion is the most earnest, he will not be able to do so.

Milarepa once asked Rongtön Lhaga, an adept of the Great Perfection, to bestow the initiation of the Great Perfection and the related pith instruction. "The Dharma I teach," Lama Rongtön Lhaga replied, "is the Great Perfection. If one meditates on it during the day, one can become a Buddha that same day; if one meditates on it during the night, one can become a Buddha that very night. Fortunate beings whose past actions have created suitable conditions do not even need to meditate. They will be liberated simply by hearing it. Since it is a Dharma for those of eminently superior faculties, I will teach it to you." Milarepa thought to himself, "It took me two weeks to obtain the main signs of success at casting spells. Seven days were enough for making hail. Now here is a teaching even easier than spells and hail—if you meditate by day you become a Buddha that day; if you meditate by night you become a Buddha that night—and if your past actions have created suitable conditions, you don't even need to meditate at all! Seeing as how I met this teaching, I obviously must be one of those whose good past actions have created suitable conditions." So, he stayed in bed without meditating. A few days later, seeing that he would not be the right master for Milarepa, Lama Rongtön Lhaga said to him, "Now I will not guide you. You should go to see Marpa, the king of translators."

Nowadays, thanks to advances in transportation and communication, studying Dharma has become more convenient. We can travel to see teachers by air or by car or learn their teachings from books, audio recordings, videos, or even online at home. In contrast, practitioners in times past had to overcome tremendous hardships to meet teachers and hear the Dharma. In the early 1950s, in order to meet his future lama Thugba Rinpoche, the then young His Holiness Jigme Phuntsok Rinpoche walked more than five hundred kilometers and crossed hills and mountains from his hometown Sertha to Dzachukha's Kyangma Ritro Monastery. Along the way, he begged for food and experienced many difficulties. At Kyangma, he studied and practiced both sutras and tantras with sheer faith and willpower despite harsh conditions. At that time, his parents had both passed away, and no one supported him with food and clothes. He lived on meager rations of yogurt provided by Kyangma. Small and shabby was his shack made of earth and thatch, unable to shield the wind. As autumn and winter advanced, he had no warm clothes to fend off the cold, and he had to dig a hole in the ground inside the shack. Filling the hole with dry straw, he sat in the hole to read as well as to keep himself warm. At night, he lit a butter lamp and stayed up to study. If he was tired, he would lean against the hole and take a small break. He was greatly inspired by the story of how the omniscient Longchenpa followed his teacher, Rigdzin Kumaradza. During the most difficult time, Longchenpa lived for two months with only three Tibetan liters of tsampa. When it snowed, he stayed in a sack made of yak hair. The sack was used as both a quilt and a mattress. Although the conditions were extremely harsh, Longchenpa persisted in learning and received many heart teachings from Rigdzin Kumaradza. He was thus called "Kunkhyen Yeni Rabjam," meaning "the omniscient master who lived in a yak-hair sack." Later, Longchenpa became the lineage holder of Rigdzin Kumaradza. Anyone who sees, hears, remembers, or encounters him will attain enlightenment.

The blessings of a teacher are omnipresent. In other words, all we experience in life is infused with the blessings of buddhas and bodhisattvas. This understanding, this trust, gives us the strength to accept every encounter in life and take everything into the path. To some people, nonetheless, "the blessings of a teacher" mean that they do not need to be troubled with mundane concerns. They desire a way or a person to lift them out of this trivial and vulgar life and take them to a wonderland. Is it good or bad that worldly matters are no longer appealing to them? If they still hope to gain certain things, achieve certain states, or maintain a certain status— whether it is about secular fame, money, love and desire, or about transcendental fame, gains, clairvoyance and meditative states—it really makes no difference. The difference, if any, is that they are simply following another way of fortifying their ego.

If you lose your job, you do not take it as your being unable, unlucky, or unskillful. Instead you see it as a test, a special ordeal given by buddhas and bodhisattvas, to let you find out whether you are able to endure life's various turns. Everything that happens in your life has its meaning. If you do believe in the omnipresence of your teacher's blessings, you can accept whatever comes, even if you are at the end of your means. And your determination and openness are more than enough to make your life rich and free.

Following your teacher, you will begin to study and contemplate Dharma. You will be fascinated and awestruck by the beauty and elegance of Buddhist classic texts, logical systems, views, concepts, and theories, as well as by the inspiring stories of accomplished practitioners. However, if you fail to integrate these things into your mind and gain insight and realization, they will become mere objects of knowledge. His Holiness Jigme Phuntsok Rinpoche often said that to learn Dharma is not for us to gather and flaunt knowledge but to liberate us from samsara. Knowledge can lend you confidence and affirmation, or be something you can show off to others, but it cannot reliably reduce your delusion. Without having firm faith in your teacher and constantly praying for their blessings, you are susceptible to a return to old habits. Your Buddhist learning becomes only an activity of hoarding knowledge and experience.

The great Indian pandita Naropa was already highly learned and recognized when one day a wisdom *dakini* told him that he was learned in words but not in their meanings. Knowing that this was his precise problem, Naropa set out to follow the great Tilopa and learned and practiced as a beginner. His confidence in Tilopa never wavered, all the pains and hardships he suffered notwithstanding. It was while under the tutelage of Tilopa that he finally realized the uncontrived truth of all phenomena. Jnanasutra and Vimalamitra, the early lineage masters of the Great Perfection, had similar experiences. Both of them were great panditas for five hundred lifetimes but unable to attain complete enlightenment. With the help of Vajrasattva (a tantric deity often associated with purification practice in tantric Buddhism), who appeared in the sky to give them guidance, both went to China to follow Sri Singha (a great master in the Great Perfection lineage). After receiving the pith instructions from Sri Singha, they attained Buddhahood at last.

Study, contemplation, and meditation are all essential to Buddhist practice. You hear and study the teachings, which are then validated by your direct experience and realization through meditation. Initially, meditation may look intriguing and mystical, fascinating you and filling you with enthusiasm. But when you eagerly ask your teacher for special methods, he will either smile or suggest prostration, mantra recitation, or other things similarly basic, plain, and boring. You may feel bewildered: Should we not do something different to attain Buddhahood? What is the link between the goal of enlightenment and prostration and mantra recitation? You start to doubt whether the teacher really wants to teach you something valuable.

This is the work of our ego. If what it wants is not gratified, it succumbs to skepticism. You want to make a difference, achieve something, and be extraordinary, all of which are only games played by your ego in order to acquire a sense of fulfillment. We are disillusioned by mundane life, so we engage in spiritual practice. If the practice fails to bring about a sense of fulfillment, we think spiritual practice probably is no more real and reliable than worldly life itself. Had we devoted the same amount of time and energy to worldly concerns, we would probably not have ended up as barehanded as we are now. So, we constantly oscillate between secular concerns and spiritual quests, without a true transformation in the way we see and do things.

Perseverance and resilience in practice are much harder than you might think. Only when we feel good about ourselves do we believe that we are on the right track. Otherwise, we might hesitate or even give up. Unfortunately, most people actually feel awful when they start practicing, and this feeling of awfulness will last for quite some time. Prior to practice, we are mentally scattered, unaware of our restlessness and rigidity. With mind training, we suddenly realize, for the first time in our lives, how chaotic our minds are. That is embarrassing and even unpalatable to many. Regardless, this is a necessary step on the path. Without accepting our wandering mental state, there can be no concentration. Initially, our mind is noisy and haphazard, like a waterfall cascading down a mountain; after a period of practice, it becomes slow and gentle like a river flowing through a plain; then it becomes like an ocean, appearing smooth from afar but undulating when observed close up; and finally it becomes like a high mountain, still, steely, utterly immovable.

So, do not perceive spiritual practice as mystical or look for something extraordinary. This is the first message that an authentic teacher will want us to understand. Not until we have gone through various ordeals do we come to understand that a humble mind is the Way itself. The teacher advises us to recite mantras, prostrate, or practice the preliminaries of the Great Perfection because he wants us to gradually let go of all kinds of haughty expectations and extravagant fancies and to experience the real taste of Buddhist practice. As the first paragraph of the *Diamond Cutter Sutra* says, the Buddha, together with his disciples, meditated in the woods outside the city of Shravasti. When mealtime came, the Buddha put on his robe and entered the city with his alms bowl to beg for food. After he returned, he ate his meal, put aside the bowl, took off his robe, cleaned his feet, rearranged his seat, and sat on it to meditate again. Simple was the life of the Buddha, who attained supreme enlightenment and was worthy of offerings from both humans and gods.

After completing several million mantra recitations and thousands of prostrations, your mind will become much quieter, even though you may still be unable to visualize vividly the detailed images of buddhas, bodhisattvas, or mandalas. You will learn to let go of hyperbolic ambitions and romantic notions of quick attainments. Practice becomes a progressive path, solid and specific, done every single day just like eating and sleeping.

The Buddha says that all sentient beings have buddha nature, which neither arises nor ceases, neither increases nor decreases. Phrases like "buddha nature," "the true nature of the mind," or "the innate mind" all point to the same thing: the thing that is immovable and inseparable from you, always, at all times. It is neither expected to arise at a future time nor will it be given to you by your teacher. What the teacher does is simply help you to cast away all the unnecessary garbage in your backpack until the real gem shows through.

When Milarepa was with Marpa, he longed for a method to turn himself into a buddha in a single lifetime. He earnestly believed that there must be a way to become a buddha in one day or one night through meditation, just as alchemy turns a stone into gold. He figured that the lama would grant his wish at once. But he could not have been more wrong about this. Although he did whatever Marpa ordered him to do, the lama, often reprimanding him or beating him, never seemed to be pleased and never taught him anything. When one day Milarepa sat and wept for the first time, utterly shattered, Marpa came to see him. "My teachings are not just idle boasting," he comforted Milarepa. "Since you obviously have extraordinary perseverance, when you put my instructions into practice, we will see if you can attain Buddhahood in a single lifetime." He told Milarepa that he would teach him a pith instruction if the latter could build a house for him. So, day in and day out, Milarepa carried earth and stones on his back to build a house while all the other students gathered to receive initiations from the lama. Each time the house was nearly finished, Marpa would beat Milarepa furiously and make him demolish whatever he had built to build a new one. An open sore appeared on Milarepa's back. Yet he was nowhere near even the faintest shadow of the Dharma he desired.

Day after day, pain and toil softened away his pride and eased his need for quick results. He no longer thought that his negative karma was easy to purify, nor did he yearn to become a buddha in his lifetime. At one point, he even intended to give up the spiritual path and was prepared to commit suicide. It was at that moment that all obstacles between him and his lama were cleared. Agreeing to teach him at last, Marpa explained to him, "In order to purify your negative karma, I ordered you to build four houses. Each of them represented one of the four enlightened activities of pacifying, enriching, magnetizing, and subjugating. I had you thrown out of the Dharma gathering and did many other seemingly unreasonable things to you. But you have never lost faith in me. This implies that your future disciples and lineage holders will possess the necessary qualities of faith, diligence, wisdom, and compassion. They will generate genuine renunciation in this life and be perseverant and assiduous on the path. They will finally attain enlightenment, and with both compassion and the power of blessings, become perfect teachers."

The teachings of the Buddha can be passed down by words, but their uncontrived meaning only exists in the minds of teachers. Its transmission only has one passage: from mind to mind. When you have dropped all your prejudice, camouflage, and wishful thinking, no longer clinging, anxious, and desirous, your mind becomes truly open. Not until then will you be able to grasp the message that your teacher has been trying to tell you.

Opening the mind is no easy task. It requires us to weaken the mental distinction between others and ourselves, which is the very foundation of our sense of being up to now. Our entire life seems to be consumed by this conceptual differentiation: this or that, good or ill, accepting or rejecting. We always associate things with concepts, and concepts with emotions and attitudes. If we are not good at differentiation, we will be perceived as intellectually inferior. As society highly prizes a discriminating mind, the distance between people gets ever wider and the world becomes ever fragmented. We see isolation through our isolated views, while the bonds between people, things, and the world recede into the distance. Consequently, we believe selfishness to be the path to success. Some people do not know how to verify their spiritual progress. If so, just ask yourself: is there still a wide mental gap between you and others, and between you and the world?

Our teacher helps us tame our discriminating mind and foster its openness. Sometimes they use fierce means like Tilopa did with Naropa. It seemed that Tilopa always abused Naropa, whereas Naropa accepted whatever his teacher did to him without a smidgen of complaint. On the one hand, Tilopa repeatedly tested the limit of Naropa's mental resilience in a way hardly acceptable to others. On the other hand, Naropa, an extraordinary disciple, repeatedly proved to his master that his mind was wide open. Such an understanding between the two inspires wonder. Naropa deserved to be Tilopa's successor. The exchange between his mind and his master's was absolute.

We may regard ourselves as already being open. But if our teacher instructs us to do something, our first reaction is still to judge, and even from time to time to hesitate or to refuse out of disapproval. It is not because we distrust the teacher, but because we are habituated to be judgmental and prone to resist if things are not to our liking. This is exactly the root of our quandary. If we are unable to be completely open and tolerant to the teacher, how could we be open and tolerant to others? It is for this reason that the teacher guides us to learn to be open and tolerant through them, to never transgress their injunctions. Emphasizing obedience is not meant to establish the teacher's authority. Rather, it is a way of cultivating our ability to accept all things calmly. Therefore, masters of the past often advised their students to act like a ferryboat that never gets tired of being called on, or an anvil ever retaining its shape while being hammered hot and cold.

The world in which we live is a web of connections, where everything is interrelated. If we can open our hearts entirely to one person, we can open it to the entire world, and if we can communicate with one person under any circumstances, we can communicate with the entire universe. We will be appreciative and respectful to everyone around us, just as we have admired and revered our teacher for years. This mental directness, openness, and humility are thanks to our teacher's efforts. By them do we realize that we can achieve what Shantideva said. We can approach every being with loving kindness and compassion and imagine that, through these kind beings, we will one day attain complete enlightenment. Step by step, our teacher help us to adjust our attitudes and transform our minds. With progress in practice, our affection and devotion to the teacher grows. The teacher is a buddha, yet they are not one of those idols in temples who sit high with golden faces. While we have the same reverence and devotion for our teacher as for the Buddha, we have the same affection and concern for the teacher as for a fellow human being. Buddhas and bodhisattvas come to this world, manifesting birth, sickness, aging, and death as well as joy and grief as ordinary humans do. All of these have deep meanings.

I visited Chengdu shortly after His Holiness Jigme Phuntsok Rinpoche's passing. Some lay practitioners came to see me and asked whether they should feel happy or sad at the news of His Holiness's passing, given that His Holiness had gone to the Pure Land. It was true that His Holiness was a buddha, and samsara and nirvana were no different to him. But to us, samsara and nirvana were two starkly distinct worlds like heaven and earth. To guide us toward liberation, His Holiness advocated rebirth in the Pure Land throughout his entire teaching life. He also manifested signs of his rebirth in the Pure Land. In his mind, there was no suffering and pain. But in our minds, His Holiness's suffering from illness and his passing away were so real. We could not bear to see his suffering, nor could we bear our own pain and grief in losing him. How could we not grieve?

Lama Ösel was Mipham Rinpoche's attendant and had followed Mipham Rinpoche for decades. As Mipham Rinpoche was in poor health, Lama Ösel often stopped visitors at the door in order not to disturb his lama. Once in a while, Rinpoche would secretively meet his guests when Lama Ösel was not around. While keeping an eye on the front door, Mipham Rinpoche would say to the guests, "We'd better hurry and not let Lama Ösel see us. Otherwise, he would be unhappy with us." It seemed that Lama Ösel, being a disciple as well as an attendant, was stern to his lama. However, his care and love for his master was too genuine and strong to pay much attention to how he was supposed to behave. And Mipham Rinpoche knew that. Before his passing, Rinpoche went to the small cabin where his loyal disciple lived to bid farewell. He also wanted to make sure Lama Ösel had clarified all issues regarding the practice. "I am an emanation of Manjushri. My coming to this world is driven by my aspiration instead of being propelled by karmic force," Rinpoche said to him. "I have never revealed my true identity, since people in the degenerate age are so distrustful and calculating. Now that I am leaving soon, I want you to know about it so that you will not be overly sad about my departure. Our parting will be temporary. You too will go to Shambhala to meet me again there, where we will no longer be separated. As you have a close connection with me by being my disciple and attendant in this lifetime, you have shared all my merit. Everything you have done at my side, even just walking, is the cause of your future attainment of Buddhahood."

It is thanks to the merit we accumulated in past lifetimes that we have the fortune to meet our teachers in this lifetime. Nonetheless, such a meeting is short. According to a popular Chinese saying, parents may have passed away before their children can repay their debt of gratitude to them. Unlike parents, teachers do not expect us to repay their kindness. But as students we should do our best to honor them by following their teachings and practicing unflaggingly. To our teachers, may we not leave too much regret.

One night I dreamed that I revisited my life thirty-three years ago, when I first arrived at the Larung Buddhist Institute. That day, His Holiness Jigme Phuntsok Rinpoche arranged a wooden shack for me to stay in. In the dream, I also saw my then young neighbor who looked exactly the same. While we walked together chatting, I suddenly saw on the ground an ornament that was usually placed on the top of a mandala. While still in the same dream, I turned into an observer of the scene. Watching the past like a show, I thought with an overpowering sense of sorrow: when this ornament was new, His Holiness was still alive and we were all very young. At that time, my life today seemed like the distant future. But now His Holiness has gone. How could all of this have happened in the blink of an eye? Thinking along those lines, I was struck by a sharp pain that pulled me out of the dream. Awakening in the dark night, tears rolled down my face. If only I could again be in the presence of my lama, even if I had to give away everything I had. Although I would still be nervous and tense when seeing him, my joy would be inexpressible.

Our teachers are here not because they yearn to stay, but because they are too compassionate to leave. They want to help, to let us know that our minds are already as luminous as theirs. When we slowly open up, we will learn to treat people and things with love and respect, and to live in harmony with ourselves, with others, and with the world around us. On each step of our journey to this openness, it is our teachers who have been with us all the time. When our hearts become gentler and our minds broader, we will truly appreciate that everything we see and encounter—even just a cool breeze—is the manifestation of our teacher's kindness and compassion.

Our time with our teachers is fleeting. So is our human life. May we always remember the kindness of our teachers and the meaning of their teachings.

PART 3

A Practical Guide for Beginners

The Daily Practice

Many of us must continue in our roles as family members and members of society after having converted to Buddhism. Regardless of the mundane parts of our life, we should set liberation from samsara as our ultimate goal. Without renouncing cyclic existence, we can never be free of suffering—we must understand that the nature of samsara is suffering, and that the main obstacles to our liberation are our habitual tendencies and karmic obstacles stemming from ignorance since beginningless time. Buddhas and bodhisattvas have taught us many ways of purifying our karma. We must put them into practice to truly benefit. As the Buddha Shakyamuni said, "I preach the way of liberation to you, but you are the master of your own liberation."

It is unrealistic for most of you to give up worldly life completely and go on retreat in a cave. Nevertheless, it is not wise either to make an excuse for not practicing because of the needs of everyday living. You should not think that everything will turn out fine and your future liberation is guaranteed once you have taken refuge in the Three Jewels. Without practicing, you are unlikely to progress on the spiritual path. However busy you might be, you should thus spend time in practice, as it is vital to your future liberation.

Generally speaking, the daily practice can be performed by following the specific instruction of your teacher or by taking consideration of your own circumstance. It normally includes meditation, visualization, scripture or mantra recitation, and so on. Scriptures and mantras are the vajra words of buddhas and bodhisattvas designed to benefit all beings. Their power to transform your mind is truly remarkable.

The daily practice usually consists of formal morning and evening sessions at scheduled times, together with the recitation of mantras or sacred names of buddhas or bodhisattvas in between. Before you begin each session, it is best to switch off your mobile phone and disconnect the landline in order not to be disturbed during practice. An ordinary mind is easily influenced by external objects. I have received incoming calls in the middle of a practice session and was torn between picking up the call and simply ignoring it. Therefore, do whatever you can to prevent distraction before starting the practice.

Several years ago, the Tashi Triling Retreat Center provided the head lama Khenpo Darsen with a mobile phone for work. But soon Khenpo said that the phone was too disturbing. He gathered monks and nuns at Tashi Triling and said, "Tashi Triling is a place for genuine practitioners. The two stewards here need mobile phones to help manage the center's activities. But others do not need mobile phones." Having said that, Khenpo broke his phone with a stone. Khenpo Darsen is an outstanding practitioner; if he thinks that mobile phones are a disturbance, we should be more cautious about using them.

In our daily life, there are many things that distract and disturb our minds. We should not think that only figures with hideous looks and vicious behavior are demons. Actually, anything that interferes with our spiritual practice and hinders our efforts toward liberation is the manifestation of the demon lord Mara, who often hides behind a deceiving veil to tempt and disturb our mind. If we cannot recognize his true face, it will be hard for us to attain liberation.

When you are ready, you may start the morning session with water and incense offerings, followed by three prostrations to buddha images. Then you seat yourself on a meditation cushion in the seven-point posture of Vairochana. The seven-point posture of Vairochana is also called the vajra crossed-leg position or the full-lotus position. If you are unable to sit in the vajra position, you can sit in the half-vajra position (the half-lotus position). The vajra crossed-leg position helps the body to quickly gain five kinds of mental or physical benefits including pliancy. The posture requires your back to be kept straight, neither bent forward nor backward so as to counter mental laxity and excitement. According to tantric teachings, when the trunk and spine are held in an upright position, the channels become straight; and when the channels are straight, the mind becomes clear. Your head should be lowered slightly, with eyes slightly open gazing at the tip of the nose. The tip of your tongue should touch the upper palate. Your shoulders should spread and rest evenly, and the arms should not touch the body. Your hands rest in your lap in the *mudra* (hand position) of equanimity, that is, the back of the right hand rests in the palm of the left hand and the two thumbs stand up and touch each other to form a triangle. Your breath should be natural and soft, without noise and barely discernable. While inhaling and exhaling gently, quiet yourself and rest your mind for a while.

The next step is to do the breath purification exercise. First, form your left hand into the mudra called "vajra fist" by pressing your left thumb on the base of your left ring finger and curling the hand into a fist, with the four fingers on the thumb. Then press the vajra fist on the artery at the base of your left thigh. Form your right hand into a vajra fist as well and use either the right index finger or middle finger to block your right nostril. Slowly inhale through your left nostril. Imagine that all the negative karma and obstructions you have accumulated throughout time turn into a black vapor, and as you slowly breathe out, they are expelled from you. Hold your visualization and breathe three times through the left nostril. Then press your right vajra fist on the base of the right thigh and block the left nostril with your left index or ring finger. With the same visualization inhale and exhale three times through the right nostril. And finally press both fists on the bases of the thighs and breathe three times through both nostrils. As there are channels related to emotions at the bases of the ring fingers and the thighs, pressing thumbs and fists there can help calm the mind further.

After the breathing exercise, start to recall what you dreamed the night before. If you did something positive in the dream, it means that you have made progress in practice, and you should be joyful and dedicate the merit to your teacher, the Three Jewels, and all beings in the six realms. If you did something negative in the dream, it shows that you are not diligent enough in practice and you should repent immediately and pray to your teacher and the Three Jewels for their help.

After this comes the practice of Guru Yoga. People often ask whether they should visualize their teacher in their normal appearance or as a particular deity when practicing Guru Yoga. The answer is subject to your faith and devotion to the teacher. If you sincerely believe, without the slightest doubt, that your teacher is a real buddha who appears in the form of a human being to help you, you may visualize your teacher in their normal appearance. If you only imagine your teacher as a buddha and still have doubt about your teacher being a real buddha, you can visualize them as a deity. Or, if you doubt your teacher is a real buddha, but visualizing your teacher's image makes you feel better, you can also visualize your teacher's image when practicing Guru Yoga.

Now visualize that your teacher, either in his normal appearance or as a particular deity, is above the crown of your head facing in the same direction as you, or in the space an arm's length above you facing toward you. Then recite the prayer of Guru Yoga, followed by the recitation of your teacher's mantra if there is one. After the recitation, visualize that the teacher is transformed into a bright orb and enters you through your head and dissolves into your heart. By wishing that you achieve the same perfect enlightenment as your teacher's, merge your mind with your teacher's mind and rest in that state of equanimity for as long as you can. Alternatively, you can visualize yourself as a bright, five-colored orb that dissolves into your teacher's heart. Then your teacher starts to ascend, higher and higher, and farther and farther away. Merge your own mind with that of the teacher and remain in this natural state for a while.

Guru Yoga is the quintessence of all Dharma practices. It is supreme and unsurpassable, directly pointing to the uncontrived nature of all phenomena. Meanwhile, it is easy to understand and can be practiced in any situation and at any time. Every morning when you wake up, visualize that your teacher, like a fish jumping out of the water, immediately comes out of a lotus at your heart and rises above your head. As you go to sleep every evening, you lie down on your right side in the position called "the sleeping lion's posture" and visualize that your teacher enters you through the crown of your head and sits on a lotus at your heart. Your teacher's body emits rays of light, illuminating you and everything around you. Whenever you are eating or drinking, visualize your teacher inside your throat and offer them your food or drink. Whenever you are walking around, visualize your teacher in the space above your right shoulder. Whenever sickness, obstacles, or other unwanted circumstances arise, think that they have been given to you compassionately by your teacher to purify your past negative actions and to help you swiftly generate bodhichitta through your own pain. Whenever you encounter good fortune, recognize this, too, as your teacher's kindness and compassion. In a nutshell, maintain the thought, all the time, in every situation, that everything you see and encounter is your teacher's manifestation that comes directly from the teacher like rays from the sun. Always keep in mind your teacher's virtues and kindness, arouse your devotion to them constantly, and pray to them fervently or recite their mantras. Believing that your teacher is inseparable from you, and you should never stop your devotion to them for even a second.

After the practice of Guru Yoga, you should start reciting prayers, sutras, and tantric texts. Usually, you may recite the following in sequence: the *Mantra for Multiplying the Merit of Recitation*, the *Verses of the Eight Noble Auspicious Ones*, *Offering and Invocation*, the *Seven-Branch Offerings*, *Taking Refuge and Bodhisattva Vow*, the *Great Cloud of Blessings*, *In Praise of Manjushri*, the *Sadhana for Invoking Shakyamuni's Blessing*, and so on. It is better for you to recite these texts using the Tibetan pronunciation and intonation with a good understanding of their underlying meaning.

Apart from the above-mentioned texts, you may also recite the *Diamond Cutter Sutra*, which is the quintessence of the Mahayana transcendental wisdom teachings. While it is extremely hard for anyone to recite even just once the entire *Large Sutra of the Perfection of Wisdom*, it takes less than twenty minutes to recite the *Diamond Cutter Sutra*, but yields equal merit. Regular recitation of the *Diamond Cutter Sutra* allows us to swiftly purify karmic obstacles as well as to enlighten our minds. Therefore, it is highly recommended that you recite the *Diamond Cutter Sutra* once a day. In addition, the profound *Heart Sutra* is even shorter. It is through the recitation of the *Heart Sutra* that some ordained practitioners realized absolute truth and displayed many incredible qualities and acts. Apart from these two sutras, the *Sutra of the Recollection of the Noble Three Jewels* reminds us of the vast merit of the Three Jewels and evokes our gratitude to them. This is the sutra frequently chanted at the beginning of Dharma gatherings at some monasteries in Tibet. In addition, recitation of *The Confession of Downfalls to the Thirty-Five Buddhas* helps us purify our negative karma of body, speech, and mind. All these sutras are short and suitable for you to recite on a daily basis. Besides, you may also recite the *Prayer of the Ground, Path and Fruition,* the *Luminous Path to Liberation*, the *Wishing Prayer of Dewachen,* and the *Guru Puja*. According to His Holiness Jigme Phuntsok Rinpoche, the supreme practice of guru puja enables practitioners to swiftly attain realization. You can practice it in the same way that you practice guru yoga.

Once the morning session is done, you may recite deity rituals and deity mantras whenever you can during the day and count your recitations consciously.

Before you start the evening session, you should again make an incense offering and prostrate. Those who make regular offerings to Dharma protectors can make the offering at that time as well. Then you recall what you have done during the day to check whether your actions were positive or negative. If they were positive, be joyful and offer the merit to your teacher and the Three Jewels; if they were negative, recite the hundred-syllable mantra of Vajrasattva to repent. As the *Words of My Perfect Teacher* says, the daily repetition of the hundred-syllable mantra 21 times will prevent the effects of one's negative karma from developing or increasing. To recite it 108 times without interruption every day will purify all negative actions done during the day. It is thus vital to integrate the recitation of the hundred-syllable mantra into your daily practice.

To conclude the practice of the day, you should recite Samantabhadra's *Aspiration to Good Actions* in order to dedicate merit and make vows. As you go to sleep, visualize that your teacher, or your teacher in the form of a deity, enters your heart through the crown of your head and shines inside you. With virtuous thoughts in your mind you can go to sleep.

Apart from the practices mentioned above, you should also meditate at least a half hour every day. The practice of meditation is simple. If you already have direct experience of the nature of the mind, you should pray to your teacher before resting your mind in its natural state for a while. When thoughts arise, you pray to your teacher again, alternating between praying and meditating repeatedly for at least a half hour. If you have not realized emptiness, you can mentally rest with confidence in the view of emptiness and alternate your meditation with prayers to your teacher. Meditating in this manner allows you to quickly obtain blessings, and to directly experience the natural state of the mind or augment your realization. This is the meditation practice instructed by His Holiness Jigme Phuntsok Rinpoche while he transmitted the Great Perfection teaching at the Larung Buddhist Institute. I advise you to follow it as well.

All of these practices constitute only the basic requirements for Dharma practitioners. Keep in mind that anything positive you do, including these daily practices, should be supported by the practice of three supreme principles: good in the beginning by arousing bodhichitta, good in the middle by holding the view of emptiness, and good in the ending by dedicating. If you persist in these daily practices, it will not take long for you to transform your mind and develop further renunciation and bodhichitta.

You may think that you are so busy with your job that it is hard for you to do these practices regularly, and that it might be more suitable for you to practice at a future time, such as after your retirement. If so, you should also ask yourself whether you are guaranteed to live till retirement or to have time to practice in the future.

At the foot of Tashi Triling once lived a brother and his younger sister and their families. The sister had three lovely children. Every time my car passed her house, the children would run out and wave to me. Several years ago, the younger sister died suddenly, and the brother came to the Larung Buddhist Institute to ask me to perform a transference ritual for her. He sobbed while telling me that he and his younger sister went together to participate in their elder sister's wedding one morning, and that shortly after their return in the afternoon, she died unexpectedly. She was only twenty-seven years old, and she did not practice much when she was alive. The only consolation for her family was that they lived close to Tashi Triling, where the sister went to turn the prayer wheels from time to time. Sadly, this is life. Impermanence will not relent, even if you are still young and want to keep living or have children to look after. So, seize the present moment and practice unflaggingly—this is what a genuine Buddhist should do.

The practices I have discussed here are all manageable even in a busy life and can be completed within an hour if performed with focus. Buddhists are people who aspire to liberate themselves and benefit others. With true renunciation, you will surely spare time to practice regardless of being busy or not. If you cannot manage to spend even an hour on practice each day, you have yet to develop genuine faith and renunciation. Without renunciation, you might practice one day and skip your practice another day. You will not be able to make much spiritual progress by the time you die, and liberation will become empty talk. No matter how much you might regret by that time, it will be too late. So, however busy you are, you must devote time every day to practice.

Guarding Your Words

As Buddhists, we must respect the karmic law of cause and effect and be cautious about what we do, say, and think in any situation. In particular, we should not judge and comment carelessly. This is especially relevant when the Sangha is involved. Without an enlightened mind, we are unable to discern if someone is spiritually accomplished or not. Even in the small valley of Larung, for example, there were, in the nineteenth century, thirteen practitioners who achieved rainbow body under Dudjom Lingpa, a master of the Great Perfection and treasure revealer. Realized practitioners continued to emerge there in the following centuries. Some of them were well known; others were hidden, or even intentionally displayed unconventional behaviors against the norms of their times. This is why we should see all phenomena with pure perception and never pass quick judgment and make irresponsible criticisms, especially when our object is the Sangha.

If you do not have confidence in a certain member of the Sangha or have a negative opinion of that person's conduct, you may choose not to follow them or you may avoid them altogether. This is my sincere advice to you.

While we are discussing this topic, I would like to share with you the story of Amo Rabtok, a monk who used to study at the Larung Buddhist Institute. At Larung, he had followed His Holiness Jigme Phuntsok Rinpoche for more than a decade and had very strong confidence in His Holiness. However, his usual behavior seemed contrary to what one would expect from an ordained monk. Day in and day out, he loitered and practiced little, causing much trouble for the stewards at Larung. Years ago, it appeared that he could no longer bear the austere life at Larung and returned to his hometown in Ganzi. There he got married and had children. His fellow practitioners thought that he had violated his vows and commitments and suffered severe downfalls. As a result, he was not only disdained by his fellow practitioners but also heavily criticized by the villagers around him.

One day he said, "If I die, I will probably die with my head going down first." He meant to say that he would not die an auspicious death but rather an ugly one. People responded satirically, "Why don't you try to die in a good way? Otherwise, you will be despised even at the time of your death." "All right then," Amo Rabtok replied. "I will do as you wish." But nobody took his words seriously.

At the beginning of 2007, Amo Rabtok suddenly felt unwell. One night he had a dream about His Holiness Jigme Phuntsok Rinpoche, who advised him to recite one hundred thousand times the *Prayer of Attaining All Accomplishments* to remove obstacles to liberation. After he completed the recitations required, he again had a dream about His Holiness, who this time said to him, "Now come join me." The next day, Amo Rabtok told his wife about the dream, alluding to the fact that he would soon leave this world. He said he had no sadness or worries and promised that he would continue to help her practice after his departure, and he urged his wife to be ordained. As for their children, he advised her to have them sent to an orphanage in Qinghai, where one of his fellow practitioners would look after them.

After he had made all the necessary arrangements for his family, he invited several monks to his home a few days later and recited the *Prayer of the Ground, Path, and Fruition* while he sat in the crossed-leg position and meditated. After the monks said the prayer, he opened his eyes and said, "Ah, how pathetic I am. I did not manage to die. Let me try again." So, the monks started the prayer again. This time, Amo Rabtok did pass away. His body remained in the sitting position for three days. On the third day, people invited a famous tulku to recite a pith instruction of the Great Perfection for Amo Rabtok. As soon as the tulku finished the recitation, there came a sudden bang as the body of Amo Rabtok fell. Over the next few days, his body shrank to a very small size, and when it was cremated, many auspicious signs appeared, signaling his spiritual attainments. It was a wonder to all those present. People who used to criticize or slander him were deeply contrite about what they said, but they missed the chance to repent in his presence.

Other examples are Tilopa, who liked to eat fish, and the eighty-four great adepts, who also manifested all sorts of eccentric or unconventional actions. Jigme Trinle Özer and Jigme Gyalwai Nyugu were Jigme Lingpa's main disciples, who practiced under Jigme Lingpa's guidance in U-Tsang (central Tibet) for several years. One day, Jigme Lingpa told them that he had taught them everything he knew, and it was time for them to leave to practice on their own and to teach others. He also said that they were unlikely to meet him again in the future. So, the two had to leave their master, albeit reluctantly. Before their departure, Jigme Lingpa advised them to request a long-life empowerment from the great yogi Chöwang Renzin Chenpo on their way home. "It will be beneficial to you," he said to his two disciples. Chöwang Renzin Chenpo, who had mastered incredibly miraculous powers, was the most recognized treasure revealer in Tibet at the time. Thus, Jigme Trinle Özer and Jigme Gyalwai Nyugu, together with another disciple of Jigme Lingpa, went to see the great yogi.

Upon their arrival, Chöwang Renzin Chenpo was busy babysitting his young, mischievous children. When he heard their request for empowerment, he shouted at them, "Haven't you seen that I can't even handle my kids? Are you here to ridicule me?" It was not until they told him that their master Jigme Lingpa instructed them to visit that the yogi finally agreed to confer on them the empowerment. Sitting on a messy pile of household items, the yogi could not find the ritual staff that he needed. So, he took a fire poker, wrapped around it a gaiter he untied from his leg, and began to bestow the long-life empowerment. In the middle of the rite, he suddenly remembered that he also needed the empowerment vase. He looked around and took a pitcher as the vase and took the liquid inside as nectar for them to drink. The three Jigmes had no doubt about their master's instruction and the blessing power of the yogi. They drank what was given to them with full confidence. Jigme Trinle Özer even took the whole pitcher and drank all the remaining water inside. It turned out that all of them attained the spiritual accomplishment of Amitayus (the Buddha of Longevity) and lived a long life. Jigme Trinle Özer later said that he would not have lived so long if he had not drunk so much nectar at the yogi's place. "Now I cannot die earlier even if I want to," he said.

It so happens that many highly accomplished practitioners may behave "improperly" in our eyes. However, our ordinary, discriminating mind cannot understand the true nature of their actions. The Jewel of the Sangha is one of the Three Jewels in which we take refuge since our spiritual friends aid us on the path to liberation. If we criticize or even defame the Sangha, our refuge vow may be transgressed. Sutras and tantras like Karma Chagme's *Wishing Prayer of Dewachen* explain in detail the dangers of defaming the Sangha. They are detrimental to our practice and will produce severely negative effects that obstruct our chances of attaining a human rebirth, let alone liberation from samsara.

It is generally unwise to speak negatively about others. As you develop your practice, carefully guard against misconduct involving the three doors of body, speech, and mind. Such discipline is essential for attaining happiness and liberation.

A Brief Teaching
on the Preliminaries of
the Great Perfection

People often ask me to transmit and confer the tantric empowerments of the Great Perfection. Within the classification of the Nyingma school, the Dzogchen teachings are the pinnacle of the Nine Vehicles, which enable ordinary people to attain supreme Buddhahood in a single lifetime. One's confidence in Dzogchen is the result of their immeasurable virtue and merit accumulated in past lives. Padmasambhava, Mipham Rinpoche, and many other great lineage masters prophesied that the Dzogchen teachings would be widespread in the degenerate age.

Traditionally, the Dzogchen teachings were conferred secretively to a small group of people in a closed event. When I was a teenager, I started the preliminary and main practices of Dzogchen under the guidance of Khenpo Tsewang Jigme in Derge. When Khenpo transmitted Padmasambhava's *Meditation on the Six Intermediate States*, only around thirty students were allowed to join. Each day, we practiced in accordance with what was taught that day. When Khenpo transmitted Longchenpa's *Treasury of the Dharmadhatu*, only seven practitioners including myself were permitted to join. Except for me, all of the other six practitioners were monks who had practiced for many years. At the time, I was too poor to afford the instruction book. So Khenpo lent his to me and asked me to practice alone without being seen. Even my recitation of the text could not be heard by others. Therefore, I often hid myself among the prayer flags to meditate and perform recitations.

Years later, when His Holiness Jigme Phuntsok Rinpoche started to transmit a Dzogchen teaching called *Jetsen Dzogpa Chenpo* at the Larung Buddhist Institute, he allowed only a handful of students to attend. His Holiness's Dharma activities had grown so fast that by the late 1990s, Larung alone had nearly ten thousand lay and ordained resident practitioners, and worldwide countless people had become his students. To allow more people to benefit from Dzogchen, His Holiness began transmitting the Dzogchen teachings to larger audiences. In one of his teachings on the *Treasury of the Dharmadhatu* at Larung, His Holiness defied tradition and conferred the teaching on a large assembly. During the teaching period, he also arranged for either a khenpo or tulku at Larung to tutor the participants after his daily session. The teaching continued for over two months, and more than sixty tulkus and khenpos acted as tutors during the period.

In retrospect, I see that what His Holiness did out of great compassion was profoundly meaningful. At the time, His Holiness said, "There were only a few masters who could transmit the pith instructions of Dzogchen. Now there are even fewer. If I do not teach the pith instructions on the staged paths of Dzogchen to larger assemblies, I am worried that Dzogchen's future dissemination might be negatively affected. I could attain the rainbow body in this life had some of my students not broken vows. But now I will likely not attain it. Even so, I have no regret." From then on, His Holiness widely disseminated the Dzogchen teachings as a part of his flourishing Dharma activities, proving the prophecies by lineage masters like Padmasambhava and Mipham Rinpoche.

It is true that many people have confidence in Dzogchen. But apart from a select few who have sharp faculties, most practitioners must begin with the Dzogchen preliminaries to lay a solid foundation.

If the foundation is not solid, one will not be able to obtain the Dzogchen empowerment, and even if one receives the empowerment, one will not benefit much from it, just as one cannot build a solid house without having a good foundation. On the other hand, if one has practiced the preliminaries well, it will not be difficult for them to realize the pristine wisdom of Dzogchen. Historically, there were many practitioners who actually attained realization in the process of practicing the preliminaries.

When His Holiness Jigme Phuntsok Rinpoche transmitted the Dzogchen teachings at Larung, he requested that the students who intended to receive them had either already completed the preliminaries, or in special circumstances, pledged to complete the preliminaries as soon as possible after receiving the empowerment and lineage teaching. This shows how critical the preliminaries are for Dzogchen practice and its realization.

The Dzogchen preliminaries comprise the ordinary outer preliminaries and extraordinary inner preliminaries. The ordinary outer preliminaries are essential to both general and tantric practices. They are divided into four parts: the difficulty of finding the freedoms and advantages, the impermanence of life, the defects of samsara, and the law of cause and effect. Together they are also called the four kinds of renunciation.

Meditating on the difficulty of finding the freedoms and advantages and on the impermanence of life helps us to let go of our desire for worldly pleasures.

In the six realms of cyclic existence, beings in the three lower realms suffer constantly without the opportunity and freedom to practice Dharma. The gods in the heavenly realm enjoy immense pleasure that distracts them completely from practice. The *asuras* in the realm of the demigods are tormented by jealousy and lack the freedom to practice as well. Only human beings have the freedoms and advantages of engaging in Dharma practice. Nonetheless, in samsara, it is extremely difficult to attain a human life. The Buddha

Shakyamuni used the metaphors of the earth of the entire universe (as the beings of the three unfortunate realms) and the earth on his fingernail (as the humans who have the freedom and advantage of engaging Dharma practice and attaining liberation) to illustrate the difficulty of attaining a human existence. You can observe this fact by comparing the number of human beings on earth with the number of animals. You will find, for example, many more insects in a clod of soil in summertime than people in the entire world. There are also even more beings in the hell realms and the realms of hungry ghosts than humans. And among humans, how many people have the freedoms and advantages of practicing Buddhism? Though many Buddhist teachers are spreading the teachings throughout the world, out of the world's seven billion people there are only several million who are Buddhists. And among the several million people, those who actually practice the Dharma for self-liberation and for benefiting others are even fewer.

A human life is not only hard to attain, it is also brief. Right from our birth, we get closer to death without any choice in the matter. In a life filled with more obstacles and hardships than good fortune, no one knows when our human existence will end. Whether we will still be alive next year—or even next month—is an unknown. I was once aboard an evening flight to a major city in Northern China. As the plane approached the airport, the passengers could see the sprawling city through the cabin window. Many passengers were thrilled by the sight of it, but my heart sank. The city had a population of nearly twenty million people. Over the next century, these people would all depart from this world. But how many of them would be able to attain the happiness of ultimate liberation when they died? The thought saddened me.

Recently, a thirty-year-old devotee came to see me. She was recently diagnosed with terminal cancer. The threat of death came so unexpectedly that she was terrified. She kept asking me, "What can I do now?" I tried my best to console her, hoping that she could undergo treatment with a positive attitude and would not lose hope. Meanwhile, I also asked her to have faith in the Dharma regardless of the progression of her disease.

Even if one's life is smooth and free of misfortunes, it lasts only a handful of decades at best. I was once visited by an old gentleman who was a famous scholar. When he lectured in a foreign country a few years ago, he came across a book on Buddhism. To his surprise, many questions to which he had been trying to find answers had already been addressed by the Buddha Shakyamuni twenty-five hundred years ago. What amazed him most was the impeccable accuracy of the prophecies about modern society made by the Buddha and Padmasambhava. "It's incredible," he said to me. "When I read these prophecies, it seemed to me that those who made them had once lived in our modern world. I have now dropped almost all worldly matters in order to practice Buddhism single-mindedly. But it might be a little late given my age. I don't know if I have enough time to achieve what I want." What he said touched me.

Some people will hold on to worldly aspirations and it is only at a later age that they start to wonder if any of them make sense. Compared to these people, however, many more will never contemplate their place in the world—where they came from, why they are here, and where they will go—even if death is around the corner. A few years ago, I passed by a small public garden where some elderly people had gathered. Among them the relatively healthy ones were playing chess or cards, while the less healthy ones could only sit in their wheelchairs and languish in the shadow of aging. It was a sad scene for me. In contrast, Buddhists will continue using the time left in their later years to practice Dharma, as they believe that their efforts will not be wasted and will benefit both this life and future lives. I know many elderly lay practitioners who started practicing the Dharma when they were young. As a result, their lives were enriched, and they are now lighthearted and at ease as they grow old.

Life is fragile and the time of death is unknown. These stories tell us that we can lose this precious human life at any time. Even if we have the good fortune of living a long life, it only lasts a handful of decades. If we use this precious existence to pursue fame and wealth and to live for earthly pleasures, liberation will be a missed opportunity. If we do not renounce worldly concerns and do not practice the Dharma now, we will be regretful at the time of death.

The ordinary outer preliminaries also concern the defects of samsara and the karmic law of cause and effect. Meditating on these two subjects helps us to eliminate desire for pleasures attained through rebirth in the higher realms.

If we fail to attain liberation in this life, we will continue transmigrating in the six realms of samsara, where the bitter coldness and heat of the hells, the thirst and hunger of the hungry ghosts, the ignorance of animals, the constant fights of the asuras, the decadence of the gods, and the suffering of birth, aging, sickness, and death of the humans are all boundless and immeasurable. Most wild animals become food for other animals right after their birth, as stronger animals prey on weaker ones for survival. In comparison, lifetimes spent in the human realm and the realm of the gods are relatively happier and more comfortable. Still, they are, in essence, suffering: the gods will fall into the lower realms at the end of their long lives and experience the suffering of their fall, whereas humans cannot escape the suffering of birth, aging, sickness, and death. There is no single place in the six realms that can bring us lasting happiness, for suffering is the nature of samsara.

Not long ago, a student from Southern China called me for help because her friend suffered from cancer and was undergoing a painful treatment in the hospital. When I talked to the patient on the phone, he said, "I never believed that life is short and full of suffering. I thought that living the way I wanted and indulging my urges were more important than anything else. I've done many bad things for money and status. But now money and status can no longer help me and I'm experiencing the painful effects of my actions alone. I started to believe in the karmic law of cause and effect and deeply regret what I did." Lying in bed, he also expressed his wish to become a Buddhist. I presided over the refuge ritual for him over the phone.

Some people asked me why they cannot remember their past lives if transmigration in samsara and reincarnation do exist. Actually, it is absurd to negate something that we have no memory of. Although none of us can perhaps remember our experience in our mother's womb, we will not deny we were there prior to our birth. Likewise, the happiness and pain we experienced when we were one or two years old were all so vivid at that time, but who is able to recall those feelings now? Evidently, our lack of associated memories is not sufficient to draw the conclusion that certain things have not occurred. Similarly, our inability to envision past or future lives does not suggest the nonexistence of reincarnation and samsara. Some people reject the notion of samsara only because they have not truly contemplated the issue. Through observation and contemplation few people can definitively negate the Buddhist view of samsara and reincarnation.

Speaking about reincarnation, I have a story to share with you. On the way to Sertha from Ganzi in eastern Tibet stands Mount Tunkok, a sacred mountain associated with Padmasambhava. According to a saying by Padmasambhava, it is auspicious to go on a pilgrimage to the mountain during the Tibetan years of the Rooster. In 2005, it was the year of the Wood Rooster and the mountain attracted a large number of devotees. Many of them saw sacred mantras that surfaced naturally on exposed rocks. There were also other auspicious signs like rainbows appearing frequently in the sky. So, one of the locals released a few dozen sheep into the wilderness. At that time, wild monkeys still inhabited the mountain. After seeing the released sheep, one of them surprisingly left his group and started to look after the sheep. At dawn he herded them up the hill and at dusk gathered them down. He was also territorial, protecting the sheep against any intruders.

The unusual occurrence was witnessed by the pilgrims, many of who believed that the monkey was the incarnation of a relative of the family that used to own the sheep. He did so out of a persistent attachment to his previous family and processions. Lerpo Dorje, a tulku from Larung, happened to be in a retreat nearby. He also saw the event and later told me, "By herding sheep every day, the monkey left me with an impression that he once owned them." I believe that a phenomenon does not occur without its causes. Although we are unable to see the hidden forces, those who have clairvoyance will be able to decipher the interdependent elements behind a particular occurrence. From the Buddhist perspective, people who are yet to realize emptiness have to continue migrating in cyclic existence. If we are still attached to this life or future lives, we are unlikely to be freed from this transmigration.

Through practicing the ordinary outer preliminaries, you will be able to generate a genuine aversion to samsara and eventually let go of the desire for worldly pleasures while single-mindedly pursuing spiritual liberation. This mental attitude is called renunciation. Once you have become a Buddhist, it does not mean that you are able to let go of your attachments to worldly things completely. Therefore, the practice of the ordinary outer preliminaries is vital to your goal. You can practice them either separately or together with the extraordinary inner preliminaries. Before practicing, you should study intensively Patrul Rinpoche's *Words of My Perfect Teacher*, whose instructions are valuable and easily understood and followed. In Tibet, beginners of the Nyingma school, including both ordained and lay practitioners, will usually study *The Words of My Perfect Teacher* and practice accordingly as the first step in their training. When His Holiness Jigme Phuntsok Rinpoche was alive, he would teach the text at Larung almost every Tibetan January (the month of miracles). I myself also studied the text dozens of times, either through reading or hearing or teaching others. I hope you read it thoroughly at least ten times in your life. This is an easy task if liberation is your aim.

Next is the practice of the extraordinary inner preliminaries, which involves taking refuge, arousing bodhichitta, meditating and reciting on the one-hundred syllable mantra of Vajrasattva, offering the mandala, and making prostrations. These are also called the five preliminaries.

Taking refuge involves pledging to have faith in Buddhism and to learn about Buddhadharma by following the Three Jewels. It is not just the gateway to all Dharma paths but the foundation of all vows and precepts. Essentially, all Dharma paths and their ultimate fruitions begin with refuge.

A lady once came to see me. She was rich and had high social status. She was also very sociable and appeared happy. But when she was alone, she felt that life was boring and that there was no happiness in it at all. "Why do I have this feeling?" she asked me. I replied, "Perhaps because you do not have a spiritual goal. You should try to cultivate faith in a spiritual path in order to enrich your mind and become more peaceful. Material life can easily make you weary, as you will get bored when your desires are satisfied and grow discontent when your desires are not satisfied. Without spiritual pursuits and beliefs, life will fall into a circle of discontentment and boredom. On the other hand, faith can help you subdue negative emotions and make your life more balanced and fulfilling."

There are also people who have followed Buddhism for a long time. Some of them regularly participate in Dharma teachings held at monasteries and can talk about Buddhist concepts in great detail. But they have not taken refuge in Buddhism. Even for people who have taken refuge, some do not understand what the Three Jewels represent in their practice. Without taking refuge in the true sense, one is not a Buddhist, no matter how profound their views might appear, how advanced their practice seems, and how wonderful their deeds are.

Before you proceed to the actual practice of taking refuge, you should first adjust your motivation. There are three levels of motivation for taking refuge. Some people take refuge for the sake of attaining the happiness of gods and men in this and future lives. This is the refuge of lesser beings. Some take refuge with the aim of attaining nirvana for themselves. This is the refuge of middling beings. Some take refuge for the sake of helping all sentient beings attain liberation and Buddhahood. This is the refuge of great beings. You should aspire for the last.

Then you place in front of you a painting of a Buddha field that has been consecrated by your teacher as the object of refuge. You visualize the celestial mansion and its resident deities as they appear on the painting, where Guru Padmasambhava is the principal deity. While doing this, you should imagine Padmasambhava as being one in essence with your own root teacher. If you do not have a qualified root teacher, you can imagine Padmasambhava as being one in essence with His Holiness Jigme Phuntsok Rinpoche.

Why should you see Padmasambhava as being one in essence with your own root teacher? There were countless buddhas who appeared and preached the Dharma, yet you failed to attain liberation due to your own karmic obfuscations. Now your teacher comes to you again, teaching and bestowing empowerment on you. From him you can learn about the methods of avoiding rebirth to lower realms and entering higher and ultimately buddha realms. In this regard, your teacher has a closer connection with you than any past buddhas, and your teacher's kindness to you is greater. Moreover, your teacher is the source of all merit and virtue. Praying to your teacher fervently and persistently with faith allows you to accumulate tremendous merit in this life. This is the reason that you should see Padmasambhava as being one in nature with your root teacher.

While visualizing in this manner, recite the refuge verse as many times as possible in each session until you have recited it at least one hundred thousand times. To complete the required practice of taking refuge, another supplementary ten thousand recitations should be added. Meanwhile, your mind should be focused while reciting. Although the quantity of your recitations is important, the associated mental qualities are even more important. Each time you recite, you should sincerely make the vow to take refuge in the Three Jewels. If you only mouth the verse but do not mean it by heart, you will not achieve the intended result. Keep your mind focused and practice diligently until you entrust yourself to the Three Jewels with total confidence and arouse the resolution of never abandoning them even at the cost of your life.

The second practice of the five preliminaries is arousing bodhichitta. After you have taken refuge, your motivation determines whether you enter the Mahayana path (the path of the Great Vehicle) or the Hinayana path (the path of the Small Vehicle). The former involves generating bodhichitta, the aspiration to benefit all beings. As Atisha said, motivation is what differentiates Mahayana from Hinayana. Bodhichitta is the very cause of Buddhahood. Without it you cannot enter the Mahayana path, nor can you have the capacity to achieve perfect enlightenment, even if your views and insights might be profound. On the other hand, with the support of bodhichitta, even to recite a mantra once sows the seed of Buddhahood. I met some Buddhists who seemed to have strong confidence in the Middle Way and the Great Perfection. However, they did not value the preliminary practices of taking refuge and arousing bodhichitta, thinking that these practices are too basic. In truth, the realization of emptiness and the practice of bodhichitta are inseparable. Without generating genuine bodhichitta in your mental continuum, you will not be able to attain the transcendent wisdom to remove attachment and attain liberation.

For most beginners, arousing bodhichitta for the sake of all beings is easy to say but hard to do. So, arousing bodhichitta should be progressive, and you should study and contemplate as well during the process.

To perform the actual practice of arousing bodhichitta, you first visualize in front of you the field of merit in a way similar to the refuge practice. Then you think:

> Of all the countless beings throughout the vast reaches of the universe, there is not a single one who has not been my parent in the course of our succession of lives. As my parents, they all have looked after me with love and kindness. Now they are floundering in samsara's great ocean of suffering because of their deep confusion and ignorance. I must attain Buddhahood to help them escape samsara as soon as possible.

You should think along those lines with sincerity.

It is usually difficult for beginners to generate bodhichitta for all beings as a result of their attachment to relatives and friends. Therefore, you can start with your relatives and friends by trying to arouse bodhichitta for them. Then you can try to arouse bodhichitta for people who are not related to you, then for the enemies who have harmed you, and finally for all beings in the six realms, hoping that they all will attain the supreme fruition of Buddhahood. With this aspiration in mind, recite the verse arousing bodhichitta as many times as possible in each session until you have recited 110,000 in total. After you have completed the required number of recitations, you should continue training your mind using this practice until genuine bodhichitta arises in your mental continuum. If you recite the verse without mental focus, you will not be able to generate genuine bodhichitta, and without bodhichitta, your realization of the Great Perfection will be impossible.

The third practice of the five preliminaries is meditating and reciting on the hundred-syllable mantra of Vajrasattva 110,000 times. The main obstacles that prevent us from realizing the absolute nature of the universe are negative actions and habits caused by our deluded mind throughout countless lives. The beings we have killed in this life are already numerous, not to mention our negative actions in past lives. "Even after millions of aeons, a being's actions will not be lost." As Patrul Rinpoche said, one will repay any life taken from others with five hundred of one's own lives. These are the vajra words of the Buddha and the lineage masters. If we do not purify our negative actions, their effects will be unbearable once they ripen. The purification process requires us first to confess. Of all the methods of purification taught by the Buddha, the best is meditation and recitation related to Vajrasattva, who is regarded as "the king of confession."

Buddhas and bodhisattvas are, in essence, the same. But since they have taken different vows and aspirations on their paths, they manifest themselves differently. Vajrasattva vowed that he would not attain Buddhahood if he could not obtain the power to purify the karmic obfuscations of those who repent by reciting his name or prayer. Given that Vajrasattva attained Buddhahood long ago, his vows and aspirations must have been realized. Purification can only take place when one has faith in Vajrasattva and is willing to practice diligently. Anyone who confesses by reciting the one-hundred-syllable mantra of Vajrasattva 100,000 times (110,000 times in the actual practice) with the four powers will be able to eliminate all karmic obfuscations. And you should have no doubt about the extraordinary power of Vajrasattva's vows and aspirations.

Here the four powers refer to the power of support, the power of regretting having done wrong, the power of resolution, and the power of action as an antidote. In brief, the power of support is to take refuge in Vajrasattva with full confidence. The power of regretting having done wrong comes from a feeling of remorse for all the negative actions one has done in the past. The power of resolution entails remembering the mistakes one has committed and resolving never to commit them again. Finally, the power of action as an antidote involves accomplishing as many positive actions as one can to counteract past negative actions. These four powers are extremely important to the confession practice. Without them as mental support, your Vajrasattva practice may help remove some of your karmic obfuscations, but you will not be able to purify all of them gathered throughout countless aeons. Moreover, the actual meditation and recitation on Vajrasattva supported by the four powers should also be accompanied by cultivating bodhichitta. If your practice is only for the sake of your own karmic purification and liberation without taking into consideration all sentient beings, your negative karma is unlikely to be removed completely.

Another relevant Vajrasattva practice is *The Wish-Fulfilling Jewel of Vajrasattva*, a mind treasure revealed by His Holiness Jigme Phuntsok Rinpoche in 1997. The actual sadhana is easy to practice. In addition, His Holiness also allowed those who have not received the related transmission and empowerment to practice it, so this sadhana is particularly suitable for beginners. If you do not have time to practice the five preliminaries, you can first practice this Vajrasattva sadhana by meditating on and reciting the heart mantra of Vajrasattva at least two million times. This helps you to lay a good foundation for further progress. Many lay practitioners have pledged to me to recite the heart mantra of Vajrasattva one hundred million times in their lifetime, so two million recitations should be easy for anyone dedicated to finding liberation.

After you have completed the practice of the five preliminaries, you should continue reciting at least 21 or 108 times the one-hundred-syllable mantra in your daily morning session. According to works like the *Words of My Perfect Teacher*, the daily repetition of the hundred-syllable mantra 21 times while meditating on Vajrasattva will prevent the effects of one's negative actions from developing or increasing; to recite the one-hundred-syllable mantra 108 times without interruption every day will purify all negative actions committed during the day. It can be said without exaggeration that meditation and recitation on Vajrasattva is the most important and lifelong Dharma practice.

The fourth practice of the five preliminaries is the offering of the mandala, which should also be made 110,000 times. The ultimate goal of Buddhist practice is to attain supreme Buddhahood for the welfare of all beings. Its fulfillment relies on the two accumulations of merit and wisdom. The Buddha taught innumerable methods through which the two accumulations could be achieved. Among them is the simple yet supreme method of mandala offering.

When you practice the offering of the mandala, the material you use will depend on your financial means. If you are well off, the mandala base that you use can be made of precious substances such as gold or silver, and the offering piles placed on the mandala base can consist of precious stones and pearls. Ordinarily, the mandala base is made of common metals and alloys while the offering piles consist of grains such as barley, wheat, or rice. As for any other practices, your motivation plays a pivotal role. If you practice the offering of the mandala for the sake of your own rewards, you may temporarily gain some worldly benefits, but your practice will not become the cause of liberation and Buddhahood since it deviates from the true sense of the Dharma. This should be kept in mind. In fact, people who truly pursue spiritual liberation need not be overly concerned with worldly rewards. If they practice and gather the two accumulations for the sake of all beings, their own fortunes and happiness in this life will come naturally with spiritual progress, just as smoke arises simultaneously when one ignites a fire.

The fifth practice of the five preliminaries is to make full-length prostrations 110,000 times. It is best to make prostrations together with the seven-branch offerings. Alternatively, you may also combine prostrations with the practice of taking refuge, as is done traditionally. That is, each time you recite the verse of taking refuge, you make one prostration simultaneously. While doing so, it is important to link your body, speech, and mind. As you physically prostrate, recite the text or prayer and focus your mind without being distracted by wandering thoughts or external objects such as sounds and forms. Do not look around simply because something happens or someone passes by you. Keeping your mind focused while prostrating allows you to quickly purify the five poisons of negative emotions—particularly pride.

At some Tibetan Buddhist monasteries, practitioners place a wooden plank on the floor and prostrate on the plank. When prostrating, friction will cause their wrists, elbows, and knees to bleed. However, I have seen some of my students placing a carpet on the floor before slowly prostrating on it. If that still did not make them feel comfortable, they would add an additional layer of quilt on the carpet. They also take frequent breaks and chat as soon as they feel a bit tired. In my view, it is impossible for us ordinary people to be spiritually accomplished without enduring hardships. Despite his profound wisdom, even the Buddha did not find a convenient way to enable us to attain Buddhahood quickly and effortlessly. He himself abdicated his crown and practiced six years of asceticism before attaining perfect enlightenment. Similarly, Milarepa achieved his supreme spiritual accomplishment through strenuous practices beyond our imagination. As their followers, we should practice without aversion to hardship, especially since our difficulties seem trivial in comparison with those experienced by our lineage masters. If we cannot endure discomfort and pain while prostrating, we should feel embarrassed.

When I am asked to transmit the lineage teachings of the five preliminaries, I usually recite the *Preliminaries of the Longchen Nyingthig from the Great Perfection* as mentioned in Patrul Rinpoche's *Words of My Perfect Teacher*, or Mipham Rinpoche's *Luminous Path to Liberation*. You may follow either of these two sadhanas if you have received the lineage transmission. Once you have completed the five preliminaries, you may proceed to the practice of Guru Yoga.

In Hinayana Buddhism, practitioners are required to see their teachers as arhats or accomplished beings, whereas in general Mahayana practice, practitioners must see their teachers as bodhisattvas who traverse the path of accumulation, the path of preparation, or the path of seeing and beyond. In the practice of the Great Perfection, however, one must see the root teacher as a dharmakaya buddha in order to attain ultimate enlightenment. This is because the realization of the Great Perfection lies in one's faith and devotion to the teacher and in the power of the blessings from the teacher. A student may be extremely smart and capable and master various sutras and tantras, but without genuine faith in the teacher as a real buddha, they will never be able to receive the teacher's most supreme blessings and realize the Great Perfection. Guru Yoga is thus a practice that enables us to strengthen our faith and devotion to our teachers. It is also a practice that best approximates the main practice of Dzogchen. Through Guru Yoga alone many practitioners have attained realization. Some of them, as I know, were barely educated or even illiterate. Nevertheless, they were able to show auspicious signs of achievement at the time of death as a result of their faith and devotion to their teachers. Therefore, in order to strengthen your faith in your teacher, you should recite the mantra of Guru Padmasambhava ten million times. In Tibet, tens of millions or even one hundred million recitations of the Padmasambhava mantra are not unusual in the practice of Guru Yoga.

The above is a brief introduction to the preliminary practices of the Great Perfection. I hope that you can complete the five preliminaries at least once in this lifetime, since doing so will bring transformation and true meaning to your life. Before you start the practice, you should study *The Words of My Perfect Teacher*, and as you practice each preliminary, you should study the relevant chapter of the text again. If you practice in this way, you will definitely make good progress on the path. Some people only flip through the book without careful study. One has to read it thoroughly in order to digest its information properly. Buddhadharma is too profound to be understood through cursory reading. You should study *The Words of My Perfect Teacher* well rather than skimming through it while doing the practice.

Some people may say that it is very hard to practice the five preliminaries, and they may never be able to complete this practice in their lifetimes. Others may say that they will not have time to practice until some time in the future, retirement for instance. As I have repeatedly said, our human life is impermanent. If you do not spend time on practice now, you may never have the chance of liberation in the future.

Lama Tsewang Chenli was my vajra brother from a county near my birthplace. Together we received the heart teachings of Dzogchen from Khenpo Tsewang Jigme, including the *Meditation on Padmasambhava's Six Intermediate States* and Longchenpa's *Treasury of the Dharmadhatu*. He also received the teachings from His Holiness Jigme Phuntsok Rinpoche. During his lifelong practice, he recited—to mention just a few—the heart mantra of Padmasambhava 100 million times, the *Confession of Downfalls to Thirty-Five Buddhas* 100,000 times, and the *Praises of Twenty-One Taras* 1.1 million times. He also performed 1.4 million prostrations and took the one-day vow 200 times. When he prostrated, he placed a wooden plank on the ground, and the repetitive friction caused by his prostrations eventually created a hole in the plank. Years later, his realization of Dzogchen was acknowledged by the late Dzogchen master Ahacheu Rinpoche. He then said to his students, "Now that I have gained control over my rebirth, I would have no fear but joy even if I were to die right now."

In late 1994, a few months before he died, the lama had a message sent to a student who was traveling, asking the student to return as soon as possible. He said to the messenger, "My student is eager to visit foreign countries. So I have a passport for him." This perplexed people, as they knew that he had none. He also looked well, so no one expected him to die soon. Several months later, the student returned. The lama gave him a copy of his memoir chronicling his personal account of the tantric practice and his devotion to his teachers, saying that it would benefit future practitioners. The same evening, he ate dinner and recited scriptures as usual, but he felt unwell the following day. At around six o'clock in the late afternoon, after taking off some clothes with the aid of his students, he sat in the lotus posture, facing west. When his students approached him again, he had passed away.

His body maintained the same sitting posture for twenty-one days after his death, and his complexion became fairer during that period. When the cremation ceremony was being held, it was a cloudless day. People noticed a white vulture circling clockwise in the sky for a long time. Not until then did they realize the meaning of the "passport" that he had mentioned. The passport was his writing, which recorded his life as a devoted practitioner. He wanted to tell people, I suppose, that if one practices like him, they will receive a "passport" to nirvana at the time of death just like he had. I share this story with you in the hope that you will believe every effort you put into practice will have a positive impact. Only people who practice unflaggingly will be able to face death fearlessly and attain ultimate liberation and happiness.

The successful completion of the five preliminaries and Guru Yoga will change your mental continuum fundamentally. At that time, you may request a qualified lineage master to bestow you the transmission and empowerment of the Great Perfection in order to perform the main practice of Dzogchen.

Becoming Realized

In 1987, on the eastern plateau of China's Mount Wutai, my root teacher His Holiness Jigme Phuntsok Rinpoche revealed the mind treasure *Meditation on Manjushri to Attain Dzogchen*. Shortly after his return, His Holiness began to transmit this precious teaching at the Larung Buddhist Institute. The lineage transmission and its related teaching lasted one hundred days and more than one thousand students participated. According to His Holiness, it was because all participants had perfectly observed vows and commitments as a result of Manjushri's blessings that this Dzogchen treasure teaching could be transmitted to a large audience. However, this kind of large gathering for the teaching would not be repeated in the future.

At the time, I was one of those students. Apart from hearing and practicing in accordance with His Holiness's pith instruction, I also acted as a tutor for some other students after His Holiness's teaching sessions. One day, Darsen, who is now the head lama at the Tashi Triling Retreat Center, came to me. With tears in his eyes, he said to me, "It is difficult to attain a human rebirth and to meet a qualified master. His Holiness is teaching this supreme practice. If I am still unable to attain realization this time, I might never have the chance of attaining it in my life." Despite years of practice, Darsen was facing obstacles that prevented him from realizing the nature of the mind. He was worried and asked me to revisit the main points of His Holiness's teaching with him. So, we reviewed His Holiness's heart advice together:

You must have confidence in your teacher, great compassion for all beings, and conviction in the karmic law of cause and effect.

Without these, you will never be able to attain realization, even if the Buddha himself were to preach the Great Perfection to you. If you acquire these, even the demon lord Mara could not entice you away from the path to enlightenment.

If you do not see your teacher as a real buddha but think that there are buddhas or bodhisattvas more enlightened than your teacher, you will never attain realization.

Before the Buddha entered nirvana, Ananda was deeply saddened and pleaded with him to live longer. But the Buddha said, "Do not grieve, Ananda. To help beings I will soon return as a teacher." Depending on the Buddha's connection with beings and their underlying karmic conditions, the Buddha appears in different forms to save them from the bitter sea of samsaric suffering. Sometimes he appears in the form of a buddha, like the Buddha Shakyamuni who turned the Dharma wheel; sometimes he appears in the form of a bodhisattva, like Manjushri or Avalokiteshvara; sometimes he appears in the form of an ordinary person, like the teachers we meet; and sometimes he even transforms himself into a bird, cow, or other animal to save those who have a connection with him. Therefore, your teacher is the buddha whom you can see with your current physical and mental capacities. Your teacher is the outer manifestation of your own inner buddha nature.

Pray to your teacher fervently and then meditate. Those who have attained realization should rest in the mind's natural state. Those who have not seen the nature of the mind should rest in the conceptual awareness that comprehends emptiness. You should alternate praying and meditating repeatedly for at least a half hour every day. It is extremely beneficial for your realizing the nature of the mind or augmenting your realization.

We have a close connection with Mipham Rinpoche. If you visualize your teachers, Mipham Rinpoche, and Manjushri as being one in essence, you will surely obtain their blessings and realization will be within reach. When I was a one-year-old and learned to say the word *mama*, I aroused uncontrived compassion. When I was around seven or eight, I attained some degree of realization of Dzogchen. But it was only after I had generated tremendous faith in Mipham Rinpoche at the age of fifteen and prayed to him fervently while reciting his *Directly Pointing to the Nature of the Mind* that I achieved complete realization of Dzogchen. I hope my personal experience can inspire you, my students. You should learn and regularly practice the methods taught by Mipham Rinpoche.

In the lineage line of Dzogchen that I hold, all the lineage masters—from Samantabhadra to Thubga Rinpoche—were real buddhas. Although I myself am an ordinary being, the lineage I have inherited is unstained, supreme, and unsurpassable. This is because I have never thought for a second that my closest root gurus Mipham Rinpoche and Thubga Rinpoche were different from the Buddha, nor have I ever displeased any teacher who conferred Dharma on me. I wholeheartedly revered and admired all of them. If you seek the Dharma of liberation, you should examine your teacher carefully before requesting his transmission of Dzogchen. If the teacher has ever displeased or even defamed his own teachers, he has contaminated the lineage and broken the precious line of transmission that is meant to be unstained. As a result, you will not be able to obtain any blessing of the lineage from him.

Darsen was concerned that he had not mastered the Five Great Treatises, and this might put him at a disadvantage in terms of realization. In fact, knowledge and realization are not the same. It is certainly beneficial to master various sutras and tantras, but this does not warrant enlightenment. The specific teachings regarding the attainment of realization can even be very simple. The teaching of *Meditation on Manjushri to Attain Dzogchen*, for instance, encompasses everything an ordinary being needs to attain Buddhahood, but it is merely five pages long. In the traditional practice of Tibetan Buddhism, if one relies on an authentic and realized teacher and has true faith and devotion to him, they can become realized at any time, in any situation.

When Patrul Rinpoche and his disciple Nyoshul Lungtok performed tantric practices at Dzachukha, they lived on only a small amount of tsampa. One day, a devotee offered them a pie made of ginseng fruits and milk. So Patrul Rinpoche said to Nyoshul Lungtok, "Let's share the pie." But Nyoshul Lungtok declined, saying, "Master, I do not need it." Patrul Rinpoche then said, "Grab me a knife and let me cut it in half. But where is its head and where is its tail?" Upon hearing this, Nyoshul Lungtok was struck by an unprecedented realization.

Jamyang Khyentse Wangpo introduced Mipham Rinpoche to the nature of the mind in a way that was equally unusual. One day, Mipham Rinpoche went to see Jamyang Khyentse Wangpo but was stopped at the gate by an arrogant guard. Pushing the guard aside, Mipham Rinpoche entered the residence by force and saw Jamyang Khyentse Wangpo sitting there with a cloak over his head. So frightened was Mipham Rinpoche that he simply lowered his head and knelt down before his master without daring to say a word. Then, all of a sudden, Jamyang Khyentse Wangpo removed the cloak from his head and slapped Mipham Rinpoche's head while shouting, "Who are you?" Instantaneously, Mipham Rinpoche became realized.

The Chinese Zen school has many similar stories related to realization. But we should not regard them as amusing anecdotes, or think that realization is so simple that one day we ourselves might attain it without the need to make an effort. Realization will not suddenly appear like a pie that falls on your head from the sky. Should you have no faith in your teacher, you will not be able to see it, even if your teacher breaks your head. While the teachings of the Great Perfection have clearly shown us a progressive path of training and realization, to make progress, we must practice accordingly. And any step we make on the path is thanks to the compassionate blessings of our teacher.

As His Holiness Jigme Phuntsok Rinpoche said:

> It is possible for tantric practitioners who have received the Dzogchen teachings to attain liberation in this life, or in the luminous intermediate state of *dharmata* after death, or the karmic intermediate state of becoming before rebirth, if they have had faith in and devotion to their teachers, kept the tantric vows and commitments, refrained from defaming Buddhadharma, and diligently practiced according to the stages of the path. If humans, animals, or beings in other realms hear the Dzogchen teachings, they will be connected with Dzogchen again between the ages of fifteen and twenty-five in the next life and attain liberation when the necessary causes and conditions come together.

PART 4

Recollections

Remembering My Lamas

In the summer of 2008, while I was recuperating from a major heart attack, I went through the audio tape recordings of His Holiness Jigme Phuntsok Rinpoche's oral teachings. Many of them were quite old, some even dating back more than two decades. As I played them again, everything about him—his kindness, his wise words, and his wit and great ease—was like a soothing fountain that warmly flowed into my heart. Memories of those passing years flooded my mind.

I had been with His Holiness for more than two decades. As his student, I was extremely eager to be around him. But whenever I was in his presence, I was too anxious to know what to do and often did not even dare to raise my head. Looking back, I sometimes wonder if I might have received more teachings from him had I not been so nervous. Nevertheless, I do not have any regrets, for my devotion to His Holiness has enabled me to obtain his complete blessings, which are the same as those of a real buddha. For a Buddhist practitioner, this is more than enough.

One of the recordings was a song chanted by His Holiness during his visit to Samye Monastery on December 25, 1988. He sang it as the familiar sights at Samye evoked the memory of his past lives:

> In the beautiful land of Oddiyana,
> In the center of the Lotus Light Palace circled by dakinis,
> Sits Guru Rinpoche, my heart's desire life after life.
> All the fortunate beings in the Glorious Copper Colored Mountain,
> Are listening to your wonderful song of liberation.

But I, who do not have such good fortune,
Have to wander in this part of the world, alone and desolate.
On the second floor of Samye Monastery,
You once preached the way of liberation.
How fearless and mighty I, your disciple Dorje Dudjom
    was back then,
Wholly unlike how I am now, old, doddering, and graceless.
Oh, my Guru Rinpoche,
With your great compassion you will never desert me.
For without you, to whom else could I turn?

Samye Monastery is no longer the same.
But I still remember where you once sat inside.
At the place where you smiled,
Only sorrow fills my memories.
Of all your ministers and disciples, and the Vidyadharas
    as many as stars,
Khandro Yeshe Tsogyal and I, Dorje Dudjom, were your
    most favorite.
But alas!
Who could ever have expected that I fell so much?
So, I beg you not to abandon me,
For I have neither abilities nor fortunes.

I vowed in your presence,
To help beings vast as space.
I shall do so without flinching, however hard it might be.
Please forgive me for what I just said.
I shall now put on the armor of Manjushri and spread the
    teachings,
To benefit all beings and to fulfill your wish.
May all that have a connection with you be reborn in
    your land,

And taste the supreme nectar of your extraordinary
   Dharma.
To help me march on, I thus pray for your blessings.

His Holiness was in tears when he sang this song, and his sobs
choked his singing. In the background there was also the weeping
of his students. When I heard the recording, tears welled up in
my eyes, too. Whenever His Holiness talked about his masters and
recalled his time with them, he became dewy-eyed and sentimental,
and we would shed tears as well.

Through his numerous incarnations, His Holiness appeared in
various emanations to benefit all beings. But he seldom revealed his
past lives. Only when he talked about his teachers did he occasionally touch on the subject. His Holiness had extraordinary faith
in Mipham Rinpoche. Although the two did not live in the same
period, they had a close connection with each other in their past
incarnations. It is well recognized that Mipham Rinpoche was an
emanation of Manjushri. In 1997, when His Holiness underwent
medical treatment in Guilin, a city in southern China, he recalled one
of his previous incarnations as Sudhana, who followed Manjushri's
advice to meet more than 110 spiritual teachers. One of the places
Sudhana went to was called the Fountain of Joy, and it was located
exactly where His Holiness stayed in Guilin. In another incarnation
of his, he visited the holy Mount Jizu with Manjushri's emanation
to meet the great Indian Buddhist master Asanga, who at that time
was practicing asceticism. When His Holiness reincarnated as Tenzin
Yuö Bumme, one of King Gesar's ministers, his then father Danma
was Mipham Rinpoche's previous incarnation. As King Gesar's
right-hand man, Danma was also the incarnation of Saraha, one
of the eighty-four great adepts in India. His Holiness's recollections
clearly showed that behind every unstained lineage lies an extraordinary connection built over many lifetimes between a master and
a student.

It was His Holiness Jigme Phuntsok Rinpoche's root lama Thubga Rinpoche that he spoke of most often. He often said that his happiest days in life were his six years of study under Thubga Rinpoche at Dzachukha's Kyangma Ritro Monastic College between the ages of eighteen and twenty-four. After the passing of Thubga Rinpoche, he had to return to Sertha, his home county. And memories and thoughts of his root lama accompanied him for the rest of his life.

And now I, too, have been left behind by my teachers. I can only revisit them in my memories.

My first teacher was Khenpo Tsewang Jigme, who also gave me my name shortly after my birth. When I was a kid, I was known for my mischievousness. I liked to play around with other kids, often causing trouble to my mother. But one day, I suddenly wanted to make a change. Uninterested in mundane skills and knowledge, I was fascinated by Buddhism. So, I went to see Khenpo Tsewang Jigme, a famous Buddhist scholar and yogi in the region, wanting to study Buddhism under him and to learn how to read and write. It was a difficult time, and Khenpo's care and guidance helped my mind to grow. More than a decade later, it was again under Khenpo's guidance that I gained some understanding of the Great Perfection.

When I studied under Tulku Gening at Tashi Monastery, Tulku told me that I had a close connection with him that was formed over many lifetimes, and that it was precisely this connection that urged me to go to Tashi Monastery when I was fourteen. I never lived with my father. Tulku adored me like his own son and gave me the fatherly love that I had missed. He offered me shelter, taught me sutras and tantras, took me to dig up medicinal herbs in the mountains, and let me lean against him to take naps. In winter, I often sat quietly at his feet, listening to his soft and melodic chanting. The kettle sizzled on the hot stove, the air was perfumed with the sweet aroma of tea, and the room was warm and cozy.

Unfortunately, those days did not last long, as Tulku passed away after less than two years. No longer having my lama and his protection, I left the monastery at the age of sixteen and traveled around in the region to continue my Buddhist study.

At that time, in the early 1980s, the religious atmosphere became less tense in Tibet. Buddhist masters were granted more latitude in giving public teachings. Whenever a famed Buddhist scholar gave a formal teaching, students would spontaneously set up tents around where the teacher lived and gather in a temporary "classroom" where the teaching took place. In the Dzarkuo region of Ganzi, I followed Khenpo Kunzang and received his teachings on *The Words of My Perfect Teacher* and *The Way of the Bodhisattva*. Being the poorest among his students, I had no decent clothes and was often hungry. Still I was happy. Khenpo did not have much either. But he often shared his food with me. Knowing that I cared about nothing other than study, he also asked other students to look after me. If I did not run errands properly, he asked them not to blame me.

A year later, after Khenpo Kunzang finished his teachings, I went to the Dzogchen Shri Singha Institute. During my study at Sri Singha, my health deteriorated severely due to a prolonged period of malnutrition and excessive study. If it were not for Khenpo Ternor's timely treatment of me, I would have died in a foreign place. Meanwhile, Khenpo Pema Tsewang also helped me greatly. It was through his recommendation that I had the chance to meet my root teacher His Holiness Jigme Phuntsok Rinpoche. At Larung, a wanderer like me finally had a home.

As a close student, I stayed at His Holiness's side for twenty-one years (from the age of twenty-one to the age of forty-two). His Holiness is the inspiration for all my awakened wisdom and compassion. I feel extremely privileged and deeply grateful to have been with him in the prime years of my life. As I have matured over time, the little renunciation and bodhichitta that I have generated and every kind thought and act of mine are all attributable to his blessings. Whenever I think of him, my heart is filled with abiding sweetness and melancholy.

His Holiness's presence always exuded an air of exceptional warmth and expansiveness. One could not help but feel the utmost respect for him. He often placed his hand on my head and gently stroked it while joking with me. He knew how nervous I was, so he tried to encourage me by being gentle and intimate. Every time he stroked my head, I would be immersed in utter joy for days afterward. Actually, even just having His Holiness in my dreams could brighten my day. But now he can no longer stroke my head and tease me. Dreams are the only place where I can meet him again.

Most of the teachers who taught me impermanence are now separated from me by impermanence. Although I am an ordinary man and do not remember my past lives, I will always remember the kindness of each and every teacher I have met fortunately in this life. My gratitude and thoughts will always be with them.

Faith

In winter's tranquility, I returned to Tashi Triling, where nights and days alternated in peaceful joy.

At the foot of the hill once lived Tulku Ghama. He used to invite His Holiness Jigme Phuntsok Rinpoche to the Yulung region and gave both basic and profound teachings on topics like the karmic law of cause and effect. But now Tulku's former residence has been remodeled and converted to a nursing home to provide the local elderly with a place to live and practice the Dharma. The bed used by His Holiness during his teachings is being kept intact in the house's assembly hall. Every time I visit there, that bed revives my many memories of His Holiness. There was a similar bed in His Holiness's residence at the Larung Buddhist Institute. His room used to be tiny, and the bed occupied more than half of the space. He often sat on it and chatted with us. And his warmth drew us closer to him.

Many villagers from nearby came to see me at the news of my return. Instead of coming up to Tashi Triling, they gathered outside the nursing home to wait for me, fearing that they might otherwise disturb me. Almost every afternoon I would go to the house, chatting with them and giving them some teachings. It was always a happy event for me to see them. Some of the villagers were even my childhood playmates and reminded me of the simple and joyful days of being a child.

As more and more people came to hear my teachings, their number swelled from dozens to more than two thousand on some days. They were all devoted Buddhists and full of affection. Reluctant to leave after my teaching, they often stayed on and stood at the roadside until I went out again to walk around the hill in late afternoon. And they would greet me with shy but big smiles before finally leaving with satisfaction. On their way home, they might chant mantras or sing a folk song, delighted with what they had just learned. The singing echoed in the valley, leaving the pale winter dusk more silent.

One evening I stepped out as usual to take a walk along the hill path. As I looked up, a round patch of cloud drifted toward me from the west. It must be the manifestation of His Holiness, I thought, who came from Amitabha's Western Pure Land to see me. He has never left me. Whenever I return here and see signs and marks left by his Dharma activities, I miss him even more.

In the spring of 1994, I accompanied His Holiness on his second teaching tour to the Tibetan regions of Amdo and Kham. As he was passing by the village where my mother lived, I wondered whether His Holiness would drop in. But it was such a wild dream that even just to think about it already made my heart pound. As His Holiness entered my mother's humble yak-hair tent and bestowed blessings and teachings on the locals who flocked there after hearing the news, I still felt like I was in a dream and almost cried for joy.

Life is indeed like an illusory dream, where nothing seems to stay the same. It has been five years since His Holiness's passing away. My mother's yak-hair tent has also been replaced by a white stupa. It stands there against the backdrop of a long and ever-changing flow of time to remind people of a great being that was once here and taught. Slowly as time goes by, this stupa will also disappear. But what will stay are our thoughts and gratitude to His Holiness.

His Holiness lived a simple life. He never liked to wear socks and shoes, and he walked barefoot year-round. At Larung, the familiar approaching of his footsteps on the hard ground was what we students eagerly waited for in the assembly hall before his teaching sessions started. Even now, whenever I recall the scene, the sound of his quick, solid footsteps still resonates.

His Holiness often gave away new clothes offered by disciples after having worn them once or twice. He also distributed all the monetary offerings made to him among Larung's monastic community. It is said that when he studied under his root lama Thubga Rinpoche at Kyangma Ritro, on several occasions he offered all his humble belongings including clothes to Thubga Rinpoche. After the offerings, he had to borrow clothes from fellow practitioners until he had money again. Later at Larung, together with his nun sister and niece, he sold all their belongings several times—except for Buddhist statues, scriptures, and bare necessities—to help the ordained residents.

His Holiness did not like to wear hats either. He only wore one if it was required for Dharma ceremonies. He once said in a teaching session that it is disrespectful to teachers and the Sangha if a monastic member wears a hat; and if one really wants to wear a hat, he should only wear the small round kind worn by Padmasambhava. After His Holiness said so, everyone at Larung stopped wearing hats. The only exception was Amo Rabtok, a carefree monk. He went to get a tailor-made one in Padmasambhava's style and put it on whenever he went out regardless of what others might say. Years later, he passed away in a sitting posture and manifested auspicious signs after death that indicated his spiritual accomplishment. This evidences the Dzogchen teaching that a practitioner can attain liberation purely through his faith in his teacher, provided the teacher he relies on holds an unstained lineage and has attained supreme realization. His Holiness is such a teacher, and we can fully entrust to him our happiness in this life and beyond.

His Holiness tirelessly guarded every kind thought and deed of his students. In 1994, when Tashi Triling was just a vacant lot on the hillside of the holy Mount Hayagriva, he came and consecrated the site after he learned that we were planning to construct a Dharma center there. On another occasion, he asked us to write down our individual wishes. Some of us wished to go on a lifelong retreat. Some wished to teach and write as a way of disseminating Buddhism. I wrote that I would do my best to benefit all beings by way of spreading the teachings. When he read our wishes, His Holiness was satisfied. "You must keep your commitments," he said with a smile. "Even after I have left this world, I will come back to make sure you are fulfilling your promises." Since then, our lives have had a purpose and we have been full of confidence, as we know His Holiness is watching, blessing, and guarding our every effort and achievement.

His Holiness is a buddha. A buddha's mind is beyond what we can fathom. What we can see and feel about him is only a tiny drop in a vast ocean that encompasses all his wisdom and compassion. Many people participated in his final cremation ceremonies at Larung and witnessed the intactness of his heart in the burning fire. After the cremation, vajra relics were found in the cremated ashes. Generally speaking, if a Buddhist practitioner keeps pure commitments and vows and practices diligently, he may achieve the stage of an arhat or a bodhisattva. Even so, only Buddhist relics but not vajra relics may appear after the cremation as he passes away. In the Buddhist context, vajra relics can only be found in the cremated ashes of a practitioner who has attained Buddhahood. It is thus neither an exaggeration nor a hypothesis to say that His Holiness is no different from any buddha. If we have faith and pray to him fervently, we will obtain his blessings no different from those of any other buddha.

Some lay practitioners have never met His Holiness, but they have great faith in him and wish to regard him as their teacher. However, when they approached a certain teacher to ask whether they could do so, they received a negative answer. The one they asked said, "Since you have never received any teachings and empowerments from His Holiness, he cannot be your teacher. But you can come to me for empowerments to establish me as your teacher." I was very sad to hear these words. It is a logical fallacy to assert that a teacher-student relationship cannot be formed if the two have never met. In our times, no Buddhist has ever met the Buddha Shakyamuni. But wouldn't it be absurd to say that the Buddha is not our teacher and we are not his students on the grounds that none of us has ever met him?

In the history of Buddhism, there have been numerous cases in which practitioners realized the nature of the mind under the spiritual guidance and blessings of masters who had long passed away. The great Dzogchen master Jigme Lingpa, for example, lived several hundred years after the omniscient Longchenpa. However, with extraordinary faith in Longchenpa, Jigme Lingpa always prayed to him whenever he practiced. This allowed him to attain complete enlightenment like his teacher through the latter's blessings. And he is recognized by the Nyingma school as a lineage master of Dzogchen subsequent to Longchenpa. Another example concerns Mipham Rinpoche and His Holiness. Although Mipham Rinpoche had passed away prior to His Holiness's birth, His Holiness had unflagging faith in Mipham Rinpoche. When he was in his teens, he recited Mipham Rinpoche's *Directly Pointing to the Nature of the Mind* ten thousand times and the prayer to Mipham Rinpoche one million times. After completing the recitations, he achieved realization of the Great Perfection.

In this context, key to a teacher-student relationship is the mind-to-mind connection between the two, for uncontrived faith can travel through time and space, and blessings from realized masters are omnipresent. Anyone who has genuine faith in His Holiness may consider His Holiness as their teacher.

A Boundless Treasure

His Holiness Jigme Phuntsok Rinpoche's life was an ever-abundant treasure, enriching anyone who had a connection with him. I was with His Holiness for more than two decades, receiving his teachings and accompanying him for various Dharma activities. Although I am neither daring nor able to fathom his wisdom and spiritual accomplishment, I had many close glimpses of his integrity, generosity, great impartiality, and pure kindness. And it is not an exaggeration to say that it will be my lifetime endeavor just to learn from him how to be a good person.

When I first arrived at the Larung Buddhist Institute, I had only forty-five Chinese yuan (less than five dollars). Without adequate financial means to support my living there, I intended only to have a private audience with His Holiness and did not expect to stay long. With his penetrating gaze, however, His Holiness seemed to know my thoughts during our first meeting. He invited me to stay on and had a small cabin with all the necessities arranged for me. Although His Holiness did not have much at the time, he often offered what he had to the needy without being asked. Busy teaching an ever-increasing number of students throughout the day, he was still attentive and thoughtful. As a good observer, he noticed every small detail of his students and gave them timely support, though seemingly in a manner casual and cursory. Poor students like me not only benefited from his teachings but also enjoyed his immense generosity and warmth.

His Holiness was a man of great courage and determination. If something had to be done for a good cause, he would do it regardless of the obstacles. Even if he was treated unfairly, he would never blame anybody, either in front of the person or behind his back. In 1985, His Holiness promoted a comprehensive purification and ethics reform in Tibetan monasteries as a corrective to breaches of vows and commitments by some monks and nuns. Although many monasteries welcomed and supported the movement, it also led to tensions and conflicts with certain groups of people who had vested interests. While disputes and troubles ensued in the following ten years, His Holiness never complained, blamed, or criticized anybody, nor did he argue with anyone or try to defend himself. He merely pressed on with what he believed to be the right thing to do. Only on one occasion His Holiness said calmly, "If we do not change the status quo of monastic society in Tibet and leave it uncontrolled without reestablishing monastic discipline, the future of Buddhism in Tibet will be doomed. For the sake of the favorable dissemination of the teachings, I will not give up even at the cost of my own life, let alone some pointless slander."

In my memory, His Holiness was exceptionally gentle and courteous with people. He joked a lot, but even when he teased or poked fun at others, they could still sense his sincere respect for them. Conscious of others' sensibilities, His Holiness would never do or say anything that might hurt others. He acted this way out of politeness and graciousness, which was an inherent part of his virtues. In his presence, the most obscure person would see their own preciousness, and the most desperate person would find hope. This is, I suppose, what majesty truly means in this world.

Perceptive of the shortcomings of his students, His Holiness nonetheless never commented on them if they were minor. He was a tolerant teacher, and sensitive to others' self-esteem. If on occasion he had to criticize a particular student, he would do it in a subtle and gentle way. Still, he would quickly feel sorry and try to comfort them with kind words. Although His Holiness was lenient in many ways,

Larung adopts rigorous ethical standards and monastic discipline to facilitate residents' Buddhist study and practice. Occasionally, residents who violated vows and commitments were penalized or even expelled. In these situations, His Holiness would always shed tears because this was the last thing he wished to see and hear. And if a steward wanted to report such an incident to him in detail, he would stop him.

At Larung, seating for His Holiness's teaching sessions followed the rule of first come, first served. The front rows were generally taken by students who arrived earliest. Even a high-status tulku had no choice but to take a backseat if he arrived late. Visitors and guest students often marveled at this practice of impartiality, which, however, was a mere reflection of His Holiness's personality. In his world, there were no real differences between people. If there was any difference at all, it was that he usually treated poor or weak students preferentially to show his encouragement to them.

His Holiness lost his father at age nine. His own tragic childhood had helped him to understand other people's insecurity and desolation in dire situations. Once when he was very young, he was bullied and beaten by some kids and ran home in a torrential downpour. At night, while his soaking clothes caused him to shiver, he thought, "My dear father has left me so early in such a miserable world." Full of sadness, he slowly fell asleep. Then he dreamed about Padmasambhava, radiant in gold. Standing in front him, Guru Rinpoche smiled and said to him, "Do not be sad, my child, and do not detest this world. When you grow up, you will help many others so that their lives will become meaningful." When he woke up in the morning, he found that all his sorrow and resentment had vanished. His own misery as an orphan made his heart bigger and warmer, and he was always eager to help and protect others. A man of immense compassion, he was like an inexhaustible treasure, open to anybody in need and touching the lives of millions.

His Holiness often said that being a good person is the foundation of Buddhist practice, as virtues are essential to spiritual development. Otherwise, spiritual practice is like a quixotic project of building mansions in the sky. Moral conduct was the only criterion that Asanga applied to determine whether to accept a student or not. Those with ethical lapses had to learn how to be a good person before starting their Buddhist study under him.

In our world, conventional ethical norms can vary. In the seventh century, the Tibetan king Songtsan Gampo issued a code of conduct consisting of sixteen specific commitments that applied to Tibetans in general. This code has become a well-accepted ethical guideline in Tibet and has been followed closely by Tibetans for more than a thousand years. For Tibetans, to be a good person boils down to one thing—to be kind. Kindness is the innermost core of a Buddhist.

In modern society, people want to be smart, competent, rich, and powerful, free to do whatever they desire. However, few want to be kind, for being kind seems to imply softness that makes one vulnerable. It is true that no one in this world welcomes pain and suffering, but being hard-hearted does not spare us from such things. It is for this reason that Buddhist practitioners choose to remain gentle and open in any circumstances. As Geshe Langri Thangpa's *Eight Verses on Training the Mind* states, "I will take defeat and misery upon myself, and give the victory and joy to others." Always considerate and caring, a kind person often endures loss and pain willingly, provided it makes others happy.

Kindness is the source of worldly and spiritual merit. In times past, when practitioners of the Kadampa school met, they would greet each other with words like "Have you been kind lately?" They would ask when meeting in the morning, "Were you kind in your dreams last night?" And they would bid each other farewell by saying, "I hope that you keep kindness in your heart." When Atisha once had an ache in one of his hands, he placed it in Dromtönpa's arms and said, "Since you have a kind heart, please bless my hand."

Being kind entails not harming others intentionally, and a kind person will always try to avoid causing others pain. Broadly speaking, not to harm means not to bring others troubles and afflictions. If certain words may displease others, they should not be said; if certain acts may trouble others, they should not be done. Despite good intentions, a kind person may sometimes still hurt others. Therefore, it is necessary for us to think twice before doing something. If our intent is good and we have tried our best, our act can still allow us to gather merit even if the result is less than satisfactory.

Being kind also means being compassionate toward all beings, wishing that all of them are happy and free of suffering, and rejoicing in others' virtuous acts. If we see others do negative things or encounter misfortune and suffering, we should not just stand by and do nothing, or rejoice in others' misery. Rather, we should do our best to prevent others from acting wrongly and help those who are experiencing difficulty. Dromtönpa's vajra brother Butopa never got angry. Whenever he met someone, he would greet them by saying, "I hope all is well with you."

A kind person will not harm animals while talking about his love for humans because his loving-kindness is extended equally to all beings. His Holiness was always sad to see animals suffering or being slaughtered, and he would use every means to save them. Inspired by His Holiness, his students are active in animal release that brings freedom, joy, and fearlessness to animals that are being saved, while at the same time instilling compassion, warmth, and confidence in those who help the release.

Kindness goes hand in hand with integrity. Kind people may not always be smart or able, but they are certainly people of decency. Although one may be clumsy and not know how to please others, they will be honest. They will respect their teacher and fellow practitioners, and their actions will not conflict with the words of their teacher. From either a secular or spiritual perspective, a kind heart is the cradle of peace and joy. Tsongkhapa once remarked that a kind person will live happily in both this and future lives. Kindness will also bring a person closer to liberation if they are resolute and steady in their practice.

If we nurture kindness in ourselves, every one of us can be a boundless treasure, just as His Holiness has shown.

Mother

My mother used to be the pillar of the family. She raised me and my four siblings in years fraught with poverty and hardship. At age fourteen, I left home for Tashi Monastery and no longer lived with her. About eighteen years later, in 1995, my mother was ordained at the Larung Buddhist Institute, together with my elder sister and two nieces. Although I was also there at the time, we seldom saw each other. Larung has stringent rules for residents and visitors. The living quarters of monks and nuns are segregated from each other, and any visit between monks and nuns within these quarters is strictly forbidden. If there was any need for discussion, we would gather in Larung's public meeting area outside the living quarters. A few years later, telephone lines became available, and then mobile phones, so we met even less.

A woman of gentle and serene nature, my mother talked little and was not fond of socializing. Whenever she had spare time, she would prefer to stay home and chant mantras. My sister and her two daughters were busy with study and practice. I occasionally called them to meet in the public area if I wanted to give something to my mother. But they rarely visited or called me. Nonetheless, the emotional bond between us remains strong, and we have always shared trust and support without the need to say much. Tibetans are, albeit wild and passionate in some ways, generally reserved when it comes to expressing affection among family members. For families like us, we associate ultimate happiness not with transitory family gatherings but with attainment of enlightenment. And we are pleased that all five of us are on that path.

My mother suffers from severe arthritis. As winter advances on the high plateau, the days turn so fiercely frosty and damp that she can barely walk, and her daily living has become tough at Larung, where the facilities are very basic. Seeing this, I suggested that she spend her winter in one of those Chinese cities where the climate is milder. Yet she continues to stay at Larung. Having lived her entire life on the Tibetan plateau, she loves the thin, crisp air, the expansive clear sky, and the down-to-earth interactions among people. She is also courteous and attentive, feeling uneasy if those around her are not taken care of. Undoubtedly, crowded urban living is burdensome and unappealing to her. So, I did not persist in persuading her further.

In recent years, I have occasionally invited my mother and my sister's family to come over for short stays at the Tashi Triling Retreat Center. It is during these periods that we enjoy some relaxing time together. The center is near my birthplace. On fine days, we sometimes visit the nearby hot spring, where we make a fire and chat over a cup of tea. Basking in the sun, we talk mostly about the old days. People and events of the past flow like a babbling stream, and I am transported back to the idle moments of childhood.

We used to move around a lot to find good pasture, sometimes to hilltops and sometimes to riversides. Of my mother's four children, I was the most mischievous, and I never tired of making trouble wherever we moved. The village kids who were similar in age either beat me or were beaten by me. Even those who were much older than I were the victims of my mischief. My misbehavior was so annoying that it seemed to be a daily ritual for my mother to wait at home for my return, and immediately upon my arrival, beat my buttocks while pulling my ear. Screaming loudly and twisting my body, I pretended to suffer from the beating and begged for her forgiveness. It usually did not take me long to make my mother loosen her grip so that I could run away again. Knowing that I was the least obedient child, my mother rarely took me with her when she visited neighbors or relatives. And if there were visitors at home, she always had to keep an eye on me, worrying that I might do something embarrassing in front of the guests.

Later I left home to study. While my mother did not need to worry about my mischievousness anymore, she missed me terribly. The thought of her beloved son's absence weighed heavily on her. She was not good with words, and all her emotions were conveyed through her big shy eyes, where tears often welled up after I left. Time had not been kind to her. Poverty, family, and years of hard work to make ends meet have turned a fair maiden into a doddering old woman, and her once bright and clear eyes have turned hazy. Only her smile remains the same as that of the shy young girl she once was.

My mother is like a mirror for me to reflect on life. When one approaches the winter of life, each step becomes fragile yet crucial, for it is so close to the end of this life, nearing the next. A cub can walk by itself in a few days after birth and live on its own shortly thereafter. But we humans are different. From birth to adulthood, it takes years of loving care for our parents to raise us. By the time we become independent, many of them are no longer young, and some might have even passed away. I am extremely indebted to my mother—not only did she give me life and raise me, but she also gave me the opportunity to look after her in her later years so that she can focus on Dharma practice without the need to worry about living necessities.

Obviously, not all people are as lucky as I am; not everyone gets the opportunity to repay the debt owed to one's parents. I know a young lama who intended to go with a friend to India to study Buddhism. Together they had less than one thousand Chinese yuan (about a hundred dollars at the time), so they decided to go all the way on foot. Unfortunately, shortly before their departure, the lama's mother fell ill. He had no choice but to postpone travel until her recovery. The delay was far longer than expected, and it was not until fourteen years later when his mother died that he finally managed to go on a pilgrimage to India's Bodh Gaya, a religious place popular among Buddhist pilgrims.

There he visited the Mahabodhi Temple, which houses the famous diamond throne called the Vajrasana. Inside the temple complex, he performed one hundred thousand full-length prostrations under the holy bodhi tree, beneath which Shakyamuni is said to have sat and attained enlightenment. The lama was away from home for three years. One of the supplications he performed was for the bestowal of the Buddha's blessing on his eighty-four-year-old father so that he would remain healthy and could meet his son again after his return from India. "In this land so ancient and holy, my heart is often filled with melancholy, for my mother and father are not here. Oh, home sweet home, it is time for me to go home."

From another perspective, the lama was still fortunate and enviable. Pilgrimage to the Mahabodhi Temple is a lifetime aspiration for many Tibetans, but only a few fortunate ones are able to accomplish it. Not only did the lama see the Vajrasana and touch the bodhi tree, but he also performed prostrations under the tree that once served as a shelter for the Buddha. The merit he accumulated has surely benefited his late mother, his father, the villagers, and those who have helped him.

I am an open-minded Buddhist and have great respect for other philosophies and faith traditions. I am always happy to further my understanding of them whenever I get the chance. However, drawing on my half-century of experience as well as that of others around me, I believe that happiness in this life and liberation in future lives can be attained under the guidance of Shakyamuni's unsurpassable teachings.

Shakyamuni's own mother, Queen Maya of Shakya, died seven days after giving birth to the Buddha and was reborn in the Trayastrimsha Heaven. It is said that gods and goddesses there live a long life and enjoy boundless pleasures in wonderful surroundings, an experience beyond what a son could ever dream to offer to his parents. Nonetheless, the realm of heavens is still within the cyclic existence that is caused by fundamental ignorance. As long as there is ignorance, suffering is unavoidable. It was for this reason that Shakyamuni visited his mother in heaven after his attainment of Buddhahood. He wanted to pay her respect but also preach the Dharma to her, for the only way to free his mother from suffering was to help her out of samsara. This is the best way to repay a mother's kindness.

Some scholars hold the view that Shakyamuni attained enlightenment through various practices in his lifetime. Others assert that he already attained Buddhahood long before he appeared in this world as Prince Siddhartha and came to this world only to demonstrate a path to enlightenment. I myself share the latter view. The life of the Buddha should inspire and encourage us, and it is for us to follow and to emulate. Although we ourselves have yet to achieve enlightenment like the Buddha, we can still help our parents and families to gain further understanding of Buddhism and do our best to facilitate their learning and practice.

From the perspective of a Mahayana practitioner, our connections and interactions with various people, regardless of their nature and quality, can all be transformed into a catalyst for enlightenment.

About the Author

KHENPO SHERAB ZANGPO is a lineage-holder in the tradition of the Great Perfection, the highest teachings of the Nyingma school of Tibetan Buddhism. A towering figure in Tibetan Buddhism, he is the author of multiple bestselling books in China, which have sold more than a million copies and earned him a reputation as one of the most influential spiritual mentor writers. He is one of the principal khenpos of the Larung Buddhist Institute of Five Sciences in Eastern Tibet, the world's largest of its kind; and for many years, Khenpo has been regarded as among the most influential spiritual mentors. Khenpo is among the most prominent heart disciples of his root teacher—His Holiness Jigme Phuntsok Rinpoche, who founded the institute in 1980. Born in 1963 to a nomadic family in Derge in Eastern Tibet, Khenpo received his Buddhist education at a young age from several accomplished masters in the region. At age sixteen, he began his formal study and practice of Tibetan Buddhism, and at the age of twenty-one, he received full and novice ordination. In the same year, he went to Larung and became a close student of Khenpo Jigme Phunstok Rinpoche. After receiving his khenpo degree at age twenty-four, he started his teaching career at Larung, lecturing students mainly on the Five Great Treatises as well as Guhyagarbha (the main tantra of Mahayoga).

Additionally, he has initiated group chantings of mantras and prayers, a practice that is regarded as greatly amplifying the power of such recitations. He's also tirelessly engaged in animal liberation practices, which have helped to preserve the lives of vast numbers of animals.

In 1995, Khenpo established the Tashi Triling Retreat Center—which has since become a renowned and sacred site of pilgrimage—and later its affiliated nursing home and hospital in Derge to aid local people and support monastic education. Apart from his Dharma activities in the Tibetan region, he teaches Dharma, gives empowerments, and guides group practices in mainland China and overseas.

What to Read Next
from Wisdom Publications

Tales for Transforming Adversity
A Buddhist Lama's Advice for Life's Ups and Downs
Khenpo Sodargye

"Khenpo Sodargye is an accomplished scholar, a renowned teacher, and an authentic upholder of the great Khenpo Jigme Phuntsok's lineage of Ngagyur Nyingma and Dzogchen teachings. I wholeheartedly recommend this book."
—Sogyal Rinpoche, author of *The Tibetan Book of Living and Dying*

Stilling the Mind
Shamatha Teachings from Düdjom Lingpa's Vajra Essence
B. Alan Wallace

"A much needed, very welcome book."
—Jetsun Khandro Rinpoche

Tibetan Buddhism from the Ground Up
A Practical Approach for Modern Life
B. Alan Wallace

"One of the most readable, accessible, and comprehensive introductions to Tibetan Buddhism."—*Mandala*

Journey to Certainty
The Quintessence of the Dzogchen View
An Exploration of Mipham's Beacon of Certainty
Anyen Rinpoche and Allison Choying Zangmo

"Remarkably accessible, this book is essential reading for anyone attempting to understand or practice Dzogchen today."
—John Makransky, author of *Awakening Through Love*

About Wisdom Publications

Wisdom Publications is the leading publisher of classic and contemporary Buddhist books and practical works on mindfulness. To learn more about us or to explore our other books, please visit our website at wisdompubs.org or contact us at the address below.

Wisdom Publications
199 Elm Street
Somerville, MA 02144 USA

We are a 501(c)(3) organization, and donations in support of our mission are tax deductible.

Wisdom Publications is affiliated with the Foundation for the Preservation of the Mahayana Tradition (FPMT).